The Ultimate Snake Owner Guide

Includes

Health & Breeding Resources

Australian Snake Facts

Kellie Ryan

http://www.pet-snake-guide.com/

product of
Strategic
Services

Some of the images in this book were provided by Morgue File dot com. Thank you

Contents

About the Author

Hi I'm Kellie Ryan

Throughout my life I have always loved Spiders and Snakes, much to my mum's horror. People seem to have an unnecessary fear of these beautiful creatures.

I come from Australia, and we have a wide range of snakes on our continent, in fact the most venomous snake in the world is found here, the Inland Taipan.

I have a sincere passion and respect for these Reptiles. I hope you enjoy what I have learnt from my experience of snakes to write about, not just from the USA perspective that most pet snake care authors have.

My trade certificate is in Horticulture Cert III in 2002, Diploma in Horticulture in 2003 and Diploma in Conservation and Land Management in 2007.

I now teach Conservation and Land Management and find it extremely rewarding. I have been a Professional Snake Catcher since 2007.

Most of my snake catching has so far been of Australian Copperheads and Eastern Brown Snakes that I have removed from residences or suburbia and returned them back into the bush scrubland that is their natural habitat.

As a conservationist I love the fact that I can do my part in protecting these beautiful Reptiles, for without them in their natural habitat we would be overrun by mice. Snakes play an important part in bush diversity.

My wish is that all snake owners become skilled at caring for their pet snakes, so that they have a chance to live a healthy and secure life in captivity, without unnecessary stress or risks to the snakes, or their owners.

To achieve this I have published my set of snake care books that teach snake owners all the essential information about pet snake care in my book **"The Ultimate Snake Owner Guide"** and snake health in my two bonus books **"How to Simply & Easily Keep Your Snake Healthy"** and even the basics of snake breeding in my book **"Successful Snake Breeding"**

Thanks
Kellie

Introduction

Unfortunately, many people are petrified of snakes. While there are some snakes that are dangerous and poisonous, many are gentle, making excellent pets. Even those that are more dangerous should not be feared, just respected. In this book, we want to focus primarily on the types of snakes that people keep for pets, along with proper care, housing, food, healthcare, breeding, and much more.

The interesting thing about snakes is that once a person understands them, he or she begins to see that just as with a dog, cat, or bird, a snake has personality, likes, dislikes, needs, and is a fascinating creature. If you already own a snake and were interested in learning more, or if you have been thinking about buying your first snake as a pet, then this book is for you.

We have conducted in-depth research coupled with personal experience to bring you a comprehensive book on which snake to buy, the proper way to house it, what it eats, health issues, handling, and much, much more. With this information, you can enjoy spending time with your snake, learning about its history and species. Without doubt, snakes are one of the most interesting and misunderstood creatures!

Keep in mind that while snakes make great pets for most people, they are not for everyone. A particular species of snake may be ideal for one family and not for another. Because snakes require unique care and handling, they should only be kept as pets by people who are committed to understanding them and meeting their needs.

For example, a constrictor type of snake is not something someone with small children or pets should consider. Additionally, just as with puppies, baby snakes will grow, becoming potentially more difficult to handle. Therefore, the handler must be prepared or the full-size snake and the various things a larger size snake brings.

It is important that you purchase the right type of snake and from a reputable source. In this book, you will learn about snakes that should and should not be kept in captivity, environmental requirements, escape proof closures and what to do should your snake get out, pet shop versus private breeder, special diets, and the list goes on. We want your snake-owning experience to be something positive and enjoyable, and with the right information, it will be.

Thank you for investing your time and money with this book. We are confident you will be enlightened after reading, becoming a more confident snake owner.

Selecting the Best Snake

Snakes first appeared in the fossil record during the day of the dinosaur. In fact, experts believe that snakes actually evolved from lizards as a means of surviving on land through bodies without legs. Many snakes are rare and endangered species, even being protected by the law.

The sad thing is that you will find some private breeders trying to sell such a snake, which is not only against the law but also not fair to the snake or pet owner. This type of snake requires exceptional care, unlike that standard snake kept as a pet. Therefore, when you get ready to select a snake, use the information in this book, coupled with your own research to know more about the breed you are considering.

Snakes that fall in the rare and endangered category should only be raised and kept by legitimate herpetologists and zoos that have the appropriate permits. The same is true for venomous snakes. While people can keep venomous snakes in captivity, these snakes should never be owned by the snake hobbyist but by a professional snake handler or breeder who understands the seriousness of a bite.

As you will discover further in this book, the best types of snakes the average snake enthusiast should keep include constrictors, which is boas, rat, milk, pythons, and so on, along with other snakes such as garter, corn, gopher, racer, etc. However, even among these snakes, the level and type of care and food varies. In fact, some of the more docile breeds of snakes can grow to very large sizes (six feet or better) so they require special housing.

When you get ready to buy your snake, you may already have a good idea of the breed you want - perhaps a friend or family member has a snake that you like. In addition, you might want a snake for the vibrant color or markings, along with activity level or size.

Tips for Choosing

While there is nothing wrong with having some ideas in mind, remember that just because a certain breed of snake was good for your friend or family member, it might not be the right choice for you. The exciting aspect of buying a snake is looking at all your options and then making the purchase. Therefore, we recommend you start first with the following:

Species

Again, remember that not all snakes are good for captivity. Therefore, spend adequate time researching all you can before making a decision.

Health

Obviously, you want to buy a healthy snake, one that has skin without wounds or sores, one with bright eyes, a snake that flicks its tongue, one that moves about with curiosity, and so on. Unfortunately, some people will find a snake that is not healthy but they buy it anyways believing they can help it. While this might be possible, it usually means a very sick or injured snake that is suffering.

Husbandry

Prior to buying any snake, learn about the specific husbandry needs of the snake, whether you can handle them now when the snake is young and when the snake matures. This would include things such as diet, heat, lighting, space, temperature, and handling.

Temperament

One of the most important things to understand is the snake's temperament. If you are buying a snake that can be handled by you and other family members, then you want a certain breed whereas if you were more interested in enjoying the snake from a distance, then you would go with a different breed.

In most cases, snakes kept in captivity should be handled regularly, which helps reduce the stress and any injury to the snake and to you. Therefore, determine what you want first. Keep in mind that certain species such as the anaconda would never have the right temperament for captivity. In addition, adults of any species caught in the wild would likely not be suitable.

Feeding

You want to consider a snake that can be fed easily and one that will be receptive to feedings. Although the Python is a great snake to keep in captivity, they are difficult feeders. If you have the time and patience to deal with this situation, fine but if not, you might go with a different species.

Note: In Australia, Large fines and 2yrs imprisonment for any person unlawfully taking any snake from wild, without appropriate registered license. As stated in Wildlife Act 1975.

Why a Snake

Although snakes are not for everyone, as you are about to discover, a snake offers tremendous value and benefit when kept as a pet.

If you or your significant other is still not convinced that a snake is the right choice, you might go over this list of benefits to help you decide.

Benefits of Owning a Snake

While there are many wonderful benefits associated with owning a snake, these are some of the best.

Easy Upkeep

For some reason, many people think that owning a snake means committing to tremendous time and effort. While some snakes do require a bit more attention and care, many are very easy to keep and to handle. The key with any snake is to establish an environment that is natural, comfortable, and safe. With this, the snake will adjust easily.

Time Investment

Unlike a dog that needs to be walked, a cat that requires a lot of petting, or a horse that must be ridden, a snake does not need exercise or an over abundance of attention. As long as they have a clean cage in which to live, food once or twice a week, and occasional handling, snakes are content.

Cost of Maintenance

The cost of your snake will depend primarily on two things – the type of snake and the pet shop or breeder from whom you buy. In America a corn or garter snake may cost just $10 while a boa constrictor could cost hundreds of dollars. However, after the initial money paid for the purchase of the snake, ongoing maintenance is very inexpensive.

In fact, experts have calculated the average cost of a snake, between $10 and $15 a month. Some snakes need a heated cage, which would run about $20 a year. For lighting, which is not mandatory, you are looking about the same. Apart from this, your snake would need bedding and food, which is also low cost. Therefore, the overall cost of keeping a snake is no big deal.

Odor

One of the problems seen with owning pets is the odor. For instance, cats have the litter box and dogs tend to pass gas. With a snake, they go to the bathroom very seldom because they only eat once to twice weekly, or less frequent, especially when mature. Because of this, snakes have little to no odor.

However, it is important that you keep the cage clean. In addition, some snakes such as the King Snake will release a substance when handled roughly or bothered. Unfortunately, this substance does not smell very good, as it is intended to dissuade predators. Even then, the odor can be washed off with no problem.

Noiseless

Snakes are quiet creatures, slinking around the cage, making virtually no noise. Now, some snakes will hiss or make small noises if spooked or threatened but other than this, you would generally only hear the sound of the bedding as the snake slithers over and through it. For people who prefer a quiet pet, the snake is the ideal choice.

Space

Generally, snakes need little room although the size of the cage would depend on the mature size of the snake, as well as the number of snakes kept. A good rule is that a 35-inch cage would easily house two Corn Snakes. Just remember that the size of the cage will change as the snake grows so you might invest in more than one.

Risk Factors

The biggest misconception associated with snakes is that they will kill you!

Yes, in the Amazon jungle where poisonous snakes abound, this would be a possibility. However, when you talk about Corn Snakes, King Snakes, and even Boa Constrictors, this is simply not the case.

Corn Snakes and King Snakes pose absolutely no threat.

Boa Constrictors when handled properly and respected are just as safe. As an example, if you had a Corn Snake or King Snake as a pet and it got out of its cage in the middle of the night, you would not have to sleep with one eye open to ensure your life were not in jeopardy.

Sure, the snake may enjoy a little time investigating the house but it would not cause you, your family, or other pets any harm. Take the Boa Constrictor as an example. If the snake were large, it could wrap around a child's neck causing injury. In addition, a Boa Constrictor could see your small family dog as a meal. Therefore, owning this type of snake simply means being responsible.

However, an adult could easily control the Boa. This snake is rear-fanged, which means it only has a small row of teeth in the back of the mouth. Therefore, even if you were to be bit, you would feel little to nothing and only see a line of small pricks on the skin.

Interest and Display

Watching a snake in its own environment is exciting and fun. Although they will usually lie around for hours, when they do move or eat, they are interesting to watch. Even when sleeping, you will find friends just standing in awe of this "wild" creature on display so calmly in your home. You will enjoy watching people watch the snake!

Snake Connections

After getting your first snake, you will soon discover a number of websites and clubs consisting of other snake owners, all sharing photos, stories, information, tips, and other information that makes being a snake owner so fun. To give you a few ideas of what to expect, I have included a list of sites in the **resources section** of this book:

Anatomy of a Snake

To better acquaint with your new snake, we want to provide you some brief information regarding its anatomy. While you will see many different sizes, colorations, and shapes, by all means, a snake is a snake.

Therefore, the information provided in this chapter would apply to any snake, not one particular species.

Understanding the Body

Below is a breakdown of the snake's body. With this information, you will understand how better your snake functions, how to handle it best, why it does certain things, and so on. As you will see from the illustration below, a snake's anatomy is comprised of many parts.

Skull

The snake's skull is quite interesting, created specifically for the way in which this reptile feeds. Since snakes do not have teeth for chewing as humans do and because they do not have any arms or legs, the food has to be swallowed in one piece.

In fact, the first time you see your snake eat, you might be a little surprised at how it literally puts the mouse or rat in its mouth and then just swallows it whole. However, the way the snake is capable of swallowing food whole is because of the bones in the skull, which are connected very loose by flexible ligaments.

Interestingly, to make its mouth open wide enough to swallow food whole, the jaw dislocated and then separates from the skull. The result is two completely separate parts of the jawbone that spread open from the chin. Then, once the food is down, the snake will do something that looks like a yawn but in reality, the snake is putting the jawbones back into place.

Teeth

Snakes actually have more teeth than mammals do. Some snakes will have up to 200 teeth, formed in two rows going along the top and bottom. However, the difference between snakes with mammals is that the teeth are actually connected to the side of the jawbone.

Even though snakes have so many teeth, they still cannot chew their food – the reason – the teeth point backwards. With the teeth in this position, the food can goes down very easily. During any time of the snake's life, should a tooth break or fall out, another tooth grows back in.

Another interesting fact about snake's teeth is that they actually shed their teeth, which means teeth are always sharp due to being new. The only difference in teeth is with Pythons, Boas, and venomous snakes, which have teeth of different sizes and lengths.

Eyes

While other vertebrates have the ability to focus on a sharp image on the retina using a special muscle that can change the shape of the lens, snakes cannot. In fact, in most snakes, this special muscle is simply not there. Therefore, snakes are not able to focus on a stationary movement and their eyesight is exceptional.

Jacobson's Organ

To assist snakes with seeing, they are created with a unique organ called Jacobson's Organ. Located in the top of the snake's mouth the flicker of the tongue is able to pick up micro-particles in the air, which are then sent to this organ, which connects directly to the snake's brain. As the brain receives the information, it is deciphered. Because of this, the snake is able to see better but they also have an exceptional sense of smell.

Brain

Similar to the brain of a bird, the only real difference is that the snake's brain does not have the enlarged cerebral hemispheres, which is part of the brain containing learning. With this being missing in s snake, you can only imagine that these are creatures of habit more than intelligence. Although they have limitations, snakes can learn, which typically relates to feeding schedule, handing regimen, environment, etc.

Lungs

A snake's lungs fit inside a long body, which means they are unique. Typically, the right lung is the largest, extending more than one-third of the body. Then the left lung is quite small, almost not ever there. Therefore, you could say in effect that snakes have one lung.

When being fed, there are times when the mouth is blocked by food, sometimes as long as an hour. While you might think the snake cannot breath, the truth is that it has the ability to take in air and blow it out by extending a very muscular portion of the windpipe known as the **Epiglottis**, which is located in the bottom of the mouth. This part of the body protrudes from under the prey, which helps the snake reach air and breath.

Heart

Snakes have a three-chambered heart and while effective, it is not as effective as the four-chambered heart seen in mammals. Blood is pumped into on top chamber, which is oxygen depleted. From there, oxygen rich blood from the lungs is pumped into the second top chamber. These chambers empty into the lower chamber, circulating throughout the body. This system of distributing oxygen is inefficient, which is why you will find snakes become tired easily, needing rest periodically.

Stomach

As you can imagine, a snake has an extremely strong and powerful snake. The stomach is very elastic to accommodate the stretching required to eat food whole.

In addition, the digestive juices are very powerful. In fact, these juices are so powerful that when a snake eats its prey, the prey is digested, teeth and bones included.

Kidneys

Snakes have exceptionally large kidneys, specifically when compared to the size of the body. Located in the abdominal area, the left kidney is located just behind the right kidney. Made to help filter out waste products from the bloodstream, the kidneys then pass this onto the **Cloaca** where the waste is eliminated.

Interestingly, while mammals excrete nitrogen waste in the form of water soluble urea, snakes actually excrete waste as crystals or uric acid. This forms as a dry, white paste, which is then expelled along with the feces. With this type of elimination process, snakes can use water very efficiently.

Cloaca

Snakes do not have separate urinary, anal, and reproductive openings in the body. Instead, these tracts all empty into a common chamber called the Cloaca. The waste material is stored in the Cloaca until time for elimination. Then, the Cloaca opens through a transverse slit located just behind the tail.

In addition, some snakes such as the King Snake are created with special glands, which also empty into the Cloaca. The substance contained in the glands is musk-like and ejected from the body when the snake feels afraid or threatened.

Hemipenes

Snakes practice internal fertilization at which time male sperm is introduced into the female's reproductive organ, called the **Cloaca**. However, the male snake does not have a penis but a pair of Copulatory organs called **Hemipenes**. During the mating season, just one Hemipenes is used with the other there just as a backup.

Skin

The snake has three layers of skin. The first layer or outer layer is shed as the snake grows. Then the second layer consists of protective keeled scales. Finally, you have the third layer, which is thick and comprised of pigmentation, giving the snake its color and pattern.

Anatomy of a Snake

Just before a snake sheds it skin, it has a dull, almost gray appearance. This appearance comes from milky liquid located between the old and new layers. Although you can see this on the entire body, the shedding is most noticeable initially on the spectacle scales covering the snake's eyes.

Then to get the shedding process started, the snake will start to rub its head against the side of the cage, rocks or branches in the cage, or anything hard. Soon, the dead outer layer will split and as the snake slithers along, the skin will begin to peel off the body. This process can take several days to complete. Once the entire outer layer is off, the snake's new skin is shiny.

The shedding action of the snake is associated with two things, growth, and hormones. Typically, your snake will shed its skin about six to eight times a year but the actual frequency will depend on a number of things to include temperature, environmental temperature, amount and frequency of feeding, activity level, injury, etc.

Additionally, the younger snake will generally shed more often in the first few years of life until reaching maturity. If your snake is healthy, the shedding process will be easy. In fact, you will notice a full piece of skin that the snake simply slithered out of but if the snake were injured, the skin would likely come off in several pieces.

If your snake were injured, then chances are after the skin is shed, you would notice some scarring,
21

which is normal. Keep in mind that as your snake sheds, it is very traumatic. You will even find that for sick snakes or those underfed, the shedding process could be delayed or not completed at all.

Typically, you would see this resulting in the snake shedding its skin in numerous pieces, often with some of the pieces staying attached to the snake until eventually rubbed off. Prior to the snake shedding, it will become quiet, usually up to two weeks. During this inactive period, the eyes will appear dull, almost white/blue in color.

Because of this, the snake cannot see as it normally would so you may notice a higher level of aggression, meaning handling during this time is not recommended. The overall skin will have a dull, lifeless appearance while underneath, there is new skin that is soft, vulnerable, and shiny.

Then approximately two weeks after the skin begins to shed, the eyes will become clear and the snake will start rubbing its body against rocks, tree branches, anything possible to help loosen and peel the skin. This process begins with the snake trying to loosen the skin area around the nose.

Once that happens, the snake will begin to slither in between tight areas to help loosen the remaining part of the skin. In fact, you might get to see the skin catch on something, as the snake literally crawls right out of its skin.

When the shedding process is fully complete, you can simply discard the tube-like skin. Or show your friends who are likely to be extremely fascinated.

You will notice a few changes in your snake to include greater activity level, defecation, and consumption of large amounts of water. The appearance of the snake will also have changed. The new skin is bright and shiny, showing off the snake's natural color and pattern.

Although some people believe snakes to be slimy, this is a misnomer. Snakes are naturally cool and dry and have almost flat or round, which creates the feel of the snake being slimy. In fact, scales are broken down in three categories, as shown below:

Smooth – Scales appear slick and shiny
Weakly Keeled – Scales appear shiny or dull, depending on the species
Keeled – Scales appear rough, typically with little to no shine

Movement

As you know, snakes have no legs. However, they are highly effective at getting around. The movement seen in snakes is known as lateral undulation, also referred to as the "serpentine movement". The way the movement works is that as the snake tightens and then relaxes muscles along each side of the body, horizontal waves are produced that travel down the entire length of the body.

23

At the same time, the snake is capable of orienting itself by making the tail push against any type of surface or resisting force to include land, trees, water, and so on. Once a snake gets moving, it can easily travel up to six miles per hour. While this type of movement is what you see with most snakes, there are a few exceptions.

As an example, many of the snakes found in tropical forests that climb trees will use concertina movements that resemble the earthworm. For this, the snake coils the tail around the tree, hooks the neck so it is higher in the tree, and then pulls the remainder of the body upward behind them.

Then you have the large Pythons that use a rectilinear locomotion type movement, performed by extending the scales on the underside of the belly, and followed by pushing against the ribs. Another type of locomotive movement is seen with the Sidewinder.

In this case, the snake actually arches the front portion of the body while hurling its head forward. When this happens, the snake will become airborne prior to touching the sand. To completely the movement, the Sidewinder brings the back part of the body so it aligns with the head. Then, the arching process starts all over again.

Digestion

To generate body heat through digestion, snakes have to depend on sunlight or in the case of captivity, artificial light. The most important time for a snake's cage to be at optimal temperature is during feeding so the mouse or rat can be digested. The same is true for females in the reproducing cycle. In fact, after feeding your snake, you may notice it heading to a warm rock where it can become warm, again to digest the food.

Most snakes will do whatever it takes to keep their body temperature around 29.4°C (85°F) during times of activity. In addition, for them to conserve heat, they will coil the body tightly, which means a small portion of the skin is exposed to the colder temperature. However, if a snake does become cold, it will often burrow down in sand, vegetation, or crevices of rocks.

Skeleton

The frame or skeleton of the snake is actually very lightweight but extremely pliable and flexible. Snakes are vertebrates, meaning they have a backbone consisting of small, interconnecting bones known as vertebrate. However, the size of the vertebrates is quite large, with a minimum of 100 although some snake species will have as many as 400 vertebrates.

Then, snakes have ribs, which are unanchored but kept in place with a breastbone. With the snake, the ribs are attached to the vertebrates, as well as other ribs via elastic muscles. With this type of construction, the snake can expand the ribcage to pass large prey down into its digestive tract. In addition, as you would see with the Ball Python, this type of design also allows the snake to coil tightly into a ball.

New Snake Owners

Please check within local state legislation for updated current snake pet listings. Here are a few from across the globe.

In this chapter, we will address the various species of snakes that make great pets, along with the reasons why. As mentioned briefly, choosing the right type of snake is important, for you, your family, and other animals in the home. Choosing the best snake for your situation will make the overall experience far more enjoyable and fulfilling. As you will see from the information below, the type of snake a person owns will depend in part on the individual's experience in handling and caring for a snake.

While other factors should be considered, we want to provide you with some options of different species for the inexperienced or new snake owner. The inexperienced snake owner is the person who has never before owned a snake, the person who has previously owned a snake but many years ago, or the person who currently has a snake in the home but who spends no time handling and therefore, does not have the comfort or knowledge factor.

For this type of snake owner, the best choices include Corn Snakes, King Snakes, and Ball Pythons. This chapter of the book will focus specifically on "beginner" type snakes, those that are easy to care for and a great choice when first getting started. These snakes are perfect choices for someone just getting started in the world of owning a snake.

Australian Approved Pet Snakes

Pythons are non-venomous and the most popular species for pets. Pythons constrict their prey as to suffocate by using the whole length of their body to coil their prey. The main diets of Pythons are mammals. There's an assortment of Pythons available in Australia under a basic license ranging from under 1mtr to 8mtrs at maturity, therefore research your options before purchase to ensure your snake is appropriate for you individual needs and housing requirements.

Interesting fact: Queensland is home to Scrub Pythons which can reach 8mtrs in length. All pythons are egg layers. Black headed Python (*Aspidites melonanocephauls*) and the Woma (*Aspidites ramsayi*) enjoy reptiles. Amethystine Python (*Morelia amethistina*) is one of the largest Pythons available as a pet reaching 8.5 meters however most are recorded at 5.5 mtrs in captivity.

Under Schedule 3 Licensing the following reptiles are allowed to be kept as pets in Victoria. Check with your local DPI or Reptile Shop for allowed Pets in your State Capital.

Amethystine Python Morelia amethistina
Beaded Gecko Lucasium damaeum
Bearded Dragon Pogona barbata
Black Rock Skink Egernia saxatilis
Black-headed Monitor Varanus tristis
Black-headed Python Aspidites melanocephalus
Bougainville's Skink Lerista bougainvillii
Boulenger's Skink Morethia boulengeri
Broad-shelled River Turtle Chelodina expansa
Burrowing Skink Lerista picturata
Burton's Snake-Lizard Lialis burtonis
Bynoe's Gecko Heteronotia binoei
Carpet or Diamond Python Morelia spilota
Central Bearded Dragon Pogona vitticeps
Central Netted Dragon Ctenophorus nuchalis
Centralian Blue-tongued Lizard Tiliqua multifasciata
Centralian Carpet Python Morelia bredli
Children's Python Antaresia children
Common or Green Tree Snake Dendrelaphis punctulata
Common Scaly-foot Pygopus lepidopodus
Cool Temperate Water Skink Eulamprus tympanum
Crested Dragon Ctenophorus cristatus
Delicate Skink Lampropholis delicate
Desert Cave Gecko Heteronotia spelea
EEastern Three-lined Skink Pseudemoia duperreyi
Eastern Water Dragon Physignathus lesueurii Lesueurii
Eastern Water Skink Eulamprus quoyii

29

Freshwater Snake Tropidonophis mairii
Garden Skink Lampropholis guichenoti
Gidgee Skink Egernia stokesii
Gilbert's Dragon Lophognathus gilberti
Gippsland Water Dragon Physignathus lesueurii howittii
Grass Skink Pseudemoia entrecasteauxii
Hooded Scaly-foot Pygopus nigriceps
Hosmer's Skink Egernia hosmeri
Jacky Lizard Amphibolurus muricatus
King's Skink Egernia kingie
Knob-tailed Gecko Nephrurus levis
Krefft's River Turtle Emydura krefftii
Lace Monitor Varanus varius
Land Mullet Egernia major
Large Blotched Python Antaresia stimsoni
Long-nosed Water Dragon Lophognathus longirostris
Major Skink Egernia frerei
Mallee Dragon Ctenophorus fordi
Mangrove Monitor Varanus indicus
Marbled Velvet Gecko Oedura marmorata
Mary River Tortoise Elusor macruros
Merten's Water Monitor Varanus mertensi
Military Dragon Ctenophorus isolepis
Narrow-banded Sand Swimmer

One of my Non- Venomous species include Australia's Children Python

Childrens Python: *Antaresia childreni*

Origin: Indigenous to Australia

30

Indigenous to Australia this Python is one of the smallest reaching at maturaty around 3feet in length. Found mostly in the Northern States of Australia from Central Western Australia, Northern Territory to Queensland.

Some adults are quiet however at feeding time they may become a striker. Feeding of pinky mice when young and as your pet grows change to Fuzzies.

Housing

The enclosure should be approximately 75L (20gallons) minimum for one snake, an aquarium or cabinet for two snakes approximately 113.5L (30 gallons) with venation and glass front is ideal. Enclosure .45m x1.2m x .3m (1.5ft deep x 4ft wide x1ft H). The enclosure must have a warm and cool side, differing in 5degress Celsius

Furnishings

Branches are extremely enjoyable to all pythons and other furnishings like toilet roll, aquarium ornaments like old ships anything the python can climb will be used. Hide areas are also appreciated. You can buy them from your reptile outlet or find some hollowed wood from around your area. Shaving on the base of your enclosure is inexpensive and easy to clean.

Climbing

The Children's python love to climb. Place some branches around your enclosure. Ensure the branches don't give your Python direct contact with the heating source if using lights as the Python can burn their skin from coiling around the lights. You can use Heat mats and add large rocks to hold the heat within the enclosure instead.

Water

A good sizes bowl off fresh water will be required. Pythons love to bathe in fresh water which aids shredding.

Food

Start you baby Python on Pinky Mice then moving to Fuzzies as your snake grows

Temperature

The Carpet Python enjoys a day temperature around 31-32 degrees C 88-90F and dropping 5degrees at night. The cooler side around 80 degrees F

Lighting

If possible natural daylight is best. If you place you enclosure where it gets covered by natural filtered light it is enough for the Carpet Python. You can purchase from your retail dealer UV light bulbs which are energy efficient for around $50 AUS.

Compared to Lizards this species of snake doesn't require a great deal of light.

Amethystine Python: Morelia amethistina

Origin: Northern Islands of Australia, Torre Straits Islands, Cape York Peninsula and East of Great Dividing Range, Papua New Guinea and Indonesia. Found in Rainforests and bush land related to Qlds Scrub Python. Scales appear to have a sheen creating an amethyst look give it meaning to the snakes name. Nocturnal Snake.

Black –Headed Python: Aspidites melanocephalus

Origin: Northern Western Australia, North of Northern Territory and Northern Queensland.

Ball Python Snake: Python regius
Origin: Central and West Africa

The Ball Python Snake is an excellent choice when first getting started. This particular snake will grow to around three to five feet, making it a smaller pet than the Corn or King Snake.

Extremely docile, the Ball Python is easy to handle and an all-around super pet. The name "Ball" Python comes from the fact that when this breed of snake feels afraid or threatened, it will roll up into a tight ball with its head safely tucked away inside the coils.

33

Younger Ball Python Snakes grow about one foot per year for three years, at which time the growing spurt slows down.

The amazing aspect of the Ball Python is that with proper care, they can live up to

50 years. However, the average age for this type of snake is generally between 25 and 30 years.

The only real, challenge of a Ball Python is that they tend to be finicky eaters, especially when caught in the wild and then brought to captivity. Therefore, we recommend you go with a captivity bred snake although expect to pay a little more.

Buying Tips

Again, to save yourself headache in trying to feed your snake, we suggest you stick with one that has been bred in captivity. Then, you want a snake with a round, well-proportioned body. The eyes should be clear and alert and the snake's vent clean.

Most importantly, check for any signs of respiratory problem, which would include the formation of bubbles around the nostril, heavy breathing, or wheezing. The snake should be alert and active, curious about you just as much as you are about him. If you handle the snake in the pet store or at the breeders, it should grip your hand or arm firmly but not so much that it is uncomfortable.

One of the risks associated with the Ball Python Snake is to eliminate any risk of disease to any existing snake at home, quarantine it for about three to six months in its own cage, and of course, have its fecal matter checked for internal parasites.

Housing

Generally, the Ball Python Snake is not overly active. Therefore, this type of snake would do fine in a 45.5 L (10G) to 90.922 L (20G) tank when young and a 136.383L (30G) tank as a mature snake. As with other types of snakes, the Ball Python will escape so make sure the cage is secure and a locking lid.

The Ball Python loves shredded bark, newspaper, or even artificial grass. If you use indoor/outdoor grass, you can simply soak it in a solution of 2 tablespoons bleach to a gallon of water, allow the grass to dry, and then replace in the cage. Just be sure you avoid cedar, which can be harmful to the snake.

Furnishings

Your snake will need a place to hide something dark and private. For this, a rock in the corner of the cage, a cardboard box, overturned flowerpot, and other similar items would be ideal.

Climbing

The Ball Python also enjoys climbing so add a piece of wood or tree branch as well.

35

Water

In addition to providing your Ball Python with a sturdy dish for drinking, it will also need a dish large enough for soaking, which is especially important during the shedding phase. If you like, you can place a second bowl of water in the cage, one fitted with a lid with a cutout hole.

With this, your snake can soak longer in privacy. Another option for helping the snake during the shedding phase would be to place moist sphagnum moss in a container with a lid, also with a cutout hole.

Food

As mentioned earlier, the Ball Python can be a fussy eater. To help encourage feeding, you need to keep the food small, which would include mice and rats. Typically, your snake will eat once a week but sometimes, it will go two, possible three.

For a young Ball Python Snake, feed it fuzzy mice once a week. Make sure you only offer killed food and if it is disinterested, dangle the mouse or rate by the tail in front of it to entice.

If you have a Ball Python that seems nervous or is not used to being handled, we recommend you move it to a separate "feeding cage". With this, the snake will begin to understand that one cage is for food and the other cage for you and your hand. The result will be handling the snake much easier.

Now, you need to understand that having a Ball Python Snake that fasts for months is common. As long as your snake is healthy, alert, active, and not losing too much body weight, it will be fine.

However, if you find your snake refusing to eat, take an inventory to see if there is something causing the problem. For instance, it could that the cage is too cool, perhaps the snake is not feeling well, or it might be handled too little or too much. Usually, a few adjustments will make all the difference.

If you have made the appropriate changes and nothing seems to work, we suggest a few tricks of the trade.

First, if you have been feeding your name white mice, switch to black or multi-colored.

Second, change the time of day in which it is fed, preferably at night.

Third, after placing a mouse or rat in the cage, cover it with a towel for privacy.

Finally, try dipping the dead mouse or rat in chicken broth. If all else fails, offer the snake a gerbil or hamster, followed by a trip to the veterinarian.

Interesting Fact: Ball Pythons digest nearly all their prey, bones etc. minimal scat

Temperature

The Ball Python likes a warm cage with temperatures between 26.6 -29.4°C (80- 85°F) during the day. In addition, this breed of snake loves having a rock as a basking spot, reaching temperatures of 32.2°C (90°F). For the temperature, you can use a heater or incandescent lighting on the top of the cage.

For the basking spot, we recommend you use a heating element underneath the cage rather than a heated rock on the inside to avoid serious burn. At night, the Ball Python likes its home a little cooler, generally around 23.8-25.5 °C (75 to 78°F) but no lower.

Lighting

Keep in mind that the Ball Python Snake is a nocturnal creature, which means it sleeps during the day and plays at night. Therefore, special lighting is not required. In addition, you want to avoid using the incandescent light at night, switching out the bulb for black, red, or blue.

Corn Snake: *Elaphe guttata*
Origin North America

One of the best choices for someone just starting out is the Corn Snake (Not in Australia), which is brilliantly colored as you can see in the photograph. This particular species is extremely docile, easy to take care of, and they remain a nice size for handling.

Keep in mind that if you are an experienced snake handler, you too can enjoy adding a Corn Snake to your collection. The only thing to remember is that Corn Snakes should be called Houdini Snakes in that they love to escape and have a natural talent for squeezing out of small spaces. Therefore, this type of snake requires a little room to roam and secure housing.

Although related to the Rat Snake, the Corn Snake lacks the brown and black coloration. Even so, the Corn Snake has beautiful colors and patterns, which makes this a visually pleasing snake to own, as well as fun. This snake comes from the southeast region of the United States, living primarily on land. The most active time of the day for the Corn Snake is at night, as well as dawn and dusk.

When full-grown, the Corn Snake will reach between three and five foot, which is considered a nice size for a beginner or intermediate handler. With a lifespan between 10 and 15 years, you can enjoy this species as a family pet for a long time.

The Corn Snake is inexpensive and being a carnivore, eats meat in the form of mice.

Buying Tips

When you visit your local pet store or breeder, there are certain things you should look for in a Corn Snake. The snake should have healthy looking flesh. This means there should be no cuts or scrapes.

However, you also want to check the skin for any signs of parasites such as ticks or mites. The eyes should be clear and alert, the vent should be clean, the tongue should flicker, and the snake should be active and alert.

Housing

Because the Corn Snake is such as great escape artist, you need a cage that is secure, one without places to squeeze out and escape. Based on the size of this snake, a 90L (20G) aquarium works exceptionally well.

To ensure proper ventilation and security, choose a vented lit with clamps. Remember, in addition to squeezing out, the Corn Snake will use its powerful nose to push lids off cages!

The great thing about snakes is that you do not have to spend a fortune on expensive bedding material. For the Corn Snake, you could use a number of things such as shredded newspaper, indoor/outdoor carpeting (which would need to be hosed off and dried at cage cleaning time), or even aspen or pine chips. Just make sure any chips are not sharp, which could puncture the skin of the snake, causing injury or infection.

The only downfall to using chips is that to ensure the snake does not accidentally eat them during feeding time, we recommend you feed the snake in a separate cage. Material you want to avoid includes cedar chips, pine shavings (different from chips), sand or soil, and corncob.

Furnishings

The Corn Snake enjoys getting out of the spotlight from time to time, which is why it will need something in its cage for privacy. This could be as simple as a cardboard box or a special item sold specifically for this purpose.

Climbing

Snakes also love to climb and explore. Therefore, provide your Corn Snake with a piece of wood, a branch, cardboard tube, or something similar, leaned against the wall of the cage so it has a place to climb and rest.

Water

Your Corn Snake will need a small water dish placed in the corner of the cage. The best option is a heavy ceramic dish that cannot be turned over.

Keep in mind that snakes will commonly use the water dish as the bathroom so it needs to be cleaned several times a day.

Additionally, snakes will slither through the bedding material and then drag their body through the water, which also causes it to become dirty.

Food

Corn Snakes eat mice and small rats but they should already be dead. For a young snake, pinkie mice would be used. Then as your snake begins to grow, you would gradually increase the size of the food.

For a young snake feedings should be two to four times a week. However, once mature your snake would likely eat just once a week and sometimes as long as 10 days.

Temperature

One of the keys to success in owning a Corn Snake is making sure the environment is comfortable. As a reptile, snakes need warmth, which can be produced with a heater.

For the Corn Snake, the ideal temperature would be anywhere between 21.1(70F) to 29.4 °C (85F). To accomplish this, use an overhead incandescent light. Just make sure the light is on the outside of the lid to avoid burns.

Lighting

The Corn Snake does not require lighting for the sake of lighting but using an incandescent light for heat will do no harm.

AUSTRALIAN SNAKE FACT
In Australia it is illegal to keep breed or trade Corn Snakes.
Fines Apply

King Snake: Champropeltis spp.
Origin: North America.

The King Snake is another docile breed that makes an excellent pet. Now, if you cannot locate a King Snake, you might look for a Milk Snake (*Lampropeltis triangulum*), which is very similar. This snake has beautiful color and pattern, being black in color with a red or deep orange ring.

While this is the standard color and pattern combination, you will find others, just as beautiful. The fascinating aspect of the King Snake is that in the wild, it will use its color and pattern to mimic the venomous Coral Snake.

The difference is that the Coral Snake has yellow bands that touch the red/orange bands whereas the King and Milk Snake has black touching the red/orange band.

Found in the south regions of Canada, in Central America, and throughout the United States, the King Snake is a wonderful choice. Keep in mind that this particular snake does grow much larger than the Corn Snake, commonly reaching up to seven feet in length.

However, the King Snake is just as enjoyable and easy to handle. For lifespan, the King Snake will live between 10 and 20 years on average. King snakes are more active at dawn and dusk.

This snake also falls within the constricting family, meaning that once it catches its prey, it will wrap its body around to suffocate prior to eating. Now, when it comes to the King Snake and small children or small animals, they generally are not interested. However, you would need to make a decision in which you are comfortable or simply keep the snake carefully caged.

Buying Tips

Whether buying your pet King Snake from a pet store or local breeder, you want to look for specific things to ensure you are buying a healthy pet. First, the snake's body should be full and round. The eyes should be clear and alert unless the snake is shedding at which time the eyes would be cloudy.

There should be no visible sign of parasites such as mites and ticks, which would be seen as dusty specks on the body. Another way to test for parasites is that after handling the snake, look at your hands, or rub them over a dark piece of paper to see if flakes fall off. The snake should be flicking its tongue and not having any sign of breathing problem.

The inside of the King Snake's mouth should be pink without any red spots or cheese-like spots, which would be an indicator of mouth rot. The outside skin or flesh should smooth without any cuts, scrapes, or sores. Make sure the snake's vent area is clean without any swelling and that it is active, moving about with trouble.

It is common to bring a King Snake home and have it feel a little restless at first. In fact, it may be difficult to handle right away so allow it a week or two to settle into its new home. If you notice the snake waving its body in the air as if trying to escape, this sign is one of stress. Therefore, place its cage in a warm, quiet place with a secure lid so it can calm down.

After a few days, offer the snake a dead mouse or rate to see if it wants to eat. We also recommend that after the snake has had a chance to settle in, you have it checked by your veterinarian or take fecal matter to the veterinarian to check for any internal parasites. With this, proper treatment can be offered, making your snake happy and healthy.

Housing

Of the utmost importance is providing your new King Snake with a stable and secure cage. These

45

snakes love to investigate and are exceptionally good at getting out through very small spaces. Therefore, in addition to the secure cage, you need a locking lid.

As mentioned earlier, King and Milk Snakes naturally eat other snakes so you want to house them separately or with like kind only. A small King Snake will need a cage about 45.5 (10G) to 90.922L (20G), whereas a mature snake will need something much larger due to their size, preferably 272.766L (60G) or more.

The larger cage for the King Snake is very important. This will ensure the snakes have adequate room for sleeping and eating but they are also an active breed so they need room to roam. Additionally, these snakes are prone to respiratory illness, which can be reduced by them having more space.

You can use several different types of materials for your snake's cage to include shredded newspaper, paper towels, or even butcher paper. In fact, until you have had the fecal matter checked for parasites, we recommend this, making clean up easier and spread of the problem less. After that, anything such as reptile bark, aspen shavings, or mulch works well.

Furnishings

The King Snake loves privacy in the form of places to hide. Therefore, a half of a coconut shell, cardboard box, an overturned flowerpot, and other similar items are perfect.

Climbing

Most snakes like to climb and the King Snake is no different. Simply place a piece of wood or tree branch in the cage, giving it something on which to climb.

Water

Use a sturdy ceramic dish for water, which will need to be changed several times a day in that this snake will defecate in the water.

Food

In the wild, the King Snake will live off amphibians, lizards, snakes, birds, and rodents. Because this type of snake eats other snakes as a regular part of its diet, and snakes larger than it, you want to cage both the King and Milk Snake along or with their own type to avoid cannibalism, as seen in this photo. In captivity, they eat mice and rats.

Temperature

Typically, the King Snake prefers a cage heated between 24.4 - 30°C or 76- 86°F degrees during the day, and 21.1 (70F) - 23.3°C (74°F) at night. You can use an under tank heater if you need to or overheat heating unit such as an incandescent light.

Again, make sure the snake cannot touch the hot light to avoid being burned. In addition, this type of snake likes humidity. For this, you can place a shallow dish of water in the cage such as the water dish, which should suffice. However, during the shedding phase, we recommend you mist your snake lightly or add a misting box into the cage, which will help it with the process.

Handling Your Snake

The great thing about handling a King Snake is that they become accustomed to being handled quickly. You simply want it to feel secure and comfortable with you so handle it with confidence and not too far off the ground should it drop.

Sometimes, the King Snake will excrete a musky like substance from the anal glands that is not very pleasant. However, this excretion is not harmful so just place the snake back in the cage and clean up the mess. As the snake becomes more and more used to being held by you, the snake will likely not excrete as much or as often.

The thing to remember about the King Snake is that it is a constrictor. Therefore, if you find your snake starting to wrap around your neck, arm, or hand, carefully start at the tail and unwrap him. The reason you start at the tail is that the head is the stronger end so as its body become loose it will naturally relax the head area.

You will also find that the King Snake, along with a few other breeds, regurgitates its food. From a human standpoint, we see this as disgusting. To avoid having food spit up on you, avoid handling the snake on the day it is fed. The snake might also regurgitate if it was fed a mouse or rat too large for its body, if the cage is too cool, of if it is feeling sick.

If you avoid handling the snake after eating, you reduce the size of the food, and bring the temperature up in the cage, but is still regurgitates, have your veterinarian perform an examination.

Other Possible Choices

In addition to the species of snakes provided above, the following are some other species that you might consider.

Garter Snake: Thamnophis spp.

Found throughout the United States, the Garter Snake is a friendly, small snake that is perfect for the first time owner. Although most will grow to about two feet, you will find some that reach up to 50 inches long.

Ground Snake: *Sonora semiannulata*

Reaching between 9 and 19 inches, the Ground Snake is found most open in dry, open areas of Oklahoma, Texas, Oregon, California, Idaho, and Texas.

Because of the size, this makes a nice starter snake.

Ribbon Snake: *Thamnophis spp.*

Located in the eastern portion of the United States, the Ribbon Snake generally grows to about 40 inches long and makes a great pet. Keep in mind that the Ribbon Snake prefers moisture and in the wild, lives in wet meadows, ponds, swamps, and even shallow streams.

Rubber Boa: *Charina bottai*

The Rubber Boa generally grows to about two to three feet and has a rubbery appearance, thus the name. Because this is a smaller boa, it would be relatively easy to handle. 22.7 (5G) -45.5L (10G) aquarium is required.

Check local and state laws for regulations for pet snake ownership within regional. Micro chipping snakes in United States has been talked about recently due to fear of introducing species into the wild by escapees.

Experienced Snake Owners

This chapter will cover several breeds of snakes that would be better suited for the more experienced owner/handler. The snakes listed in this section are still wonderful animals, many very tame. The difference is that these snakes tend to be larger, stronger, and therefore, require a little more attention and care.

Boa Constrictor Snake Boa constrictor

When you hear the words "boa constrictor", you generally think of this as being one breed. However, there are several subspecies of boa constrictor from which to choose. Even so, the one we want to focus on here is the Red Tailed Boa, which is easy to find, fun to own, and a great family pet.

The most important factor associated with owning any type of boa constrictor is that these snakes are strong. In fact, depending on the species, they can easily reach 10 foot or longer, reaching weights up to 22.73kg -50 pounds and sometimes, more. Take the Red Tailed Boa as an example. This particular snake will grow to around 8 to 10 feet and weigh between 45 and 50 feet. Because of this, it takes an experienced handler.

All boa constrictors are muscular and powerful. Although they are typically docile, because of the strength and natural instinct to wrap itself around prey and suffocate, they can cause harm. For this reason, we recommend boa constrictors not be kept as pets in homes with small children or small pets.

If you decide you want a boa, just make sure you have a locking cage and that kids are taught the importance of leaving the snake alone. Remember, even adults can be seriously injured by the sheer power of the boa. In addition, due to the size and power of the boa constrictor, you would generally need two people to handle it.

Even if you were strong enough, to handle it, when you get a 10-foot snake, having a second person around is always a good idea. We recommend you choose a snake that has been bred in captivity, meaning it will likely be more docile. These snakes fall under the Convention of the International Trade of Endangered Species or CITES, and even listed on the "threatened in their own habitat" list.

What does this mean to you? It means when you buy a captive bred boa, the pet store or breeder is required by law to have a permit. However, it also means that as the buyer, you too must obtain a permit. Since boa constrictors are bred freely in the United States, finding a healthy snake should never be a problem.

Buying Tips

When buying a boa constrictor of any species, you want to look for a number of things. For one thing, the snake should be alert and active, interested in why you are looking at him.

The snake's body should be muscular, firm, and full-bodied without any loose folds of skin. The eyes should be bright and alert and its tongue should be flicking.

If the snake has recently shed, make sure there are no signs of remaining shed around the eyes or tail. You also want to look for any visible parasites, make sure the snake's vent is clean, and check the skin for any cuts, scrapes, or other types of wounds.

When you pick the snake up, it should react at first by coiling its body firmly but not too strong around your arm or hand. Then, you should notice in a few minutes, its body starting to relax.

The other consideration when you purchase a large boa constrictor is the place from which the snake is purchased. Buying a boa that has been bred and raised in captivity will generally be less nervous and easier to handle.

Then, you need to remember that boa constrictors live a long time so you should have a backup plan in place should something ever happen to you where you are no longer able to care for the snake.

Finally, boa constrictors are prone to a type of disease called Inclusive Body. This virus is fatal in both boas and pythons.

The problem is that being able to tell if your snake has been exposed to this deadly disease. Understanding this disease and knowing what to look for is crucial.

Making it even more difficult is that the symptoms of the disease can take several months to appear, which are addressed in the Health Section of this book.

For this reason, all boa constrictors should be quarantined for three to six months if you have other snakes and always wash your hands with an antibacterial soap when handling one snake to the next snake.

Housing

Baby boa constrictors can be kept in a smaller, glass aquarium but for the larger, mature snakes, you want a specially made cage. The reason goes back to the overall strength of the large snake.

If the cage is not designed specifically for a boa, the cage could easily break. Therefore, you want a commercially made cage that measures about eight feet long, three foot wide, and three foot tall.

As you can imagine, a cage such as this is going to take up about 10 square feet of floor space so you will need to ensure you have adequate room to house a snake such as this.

Because of the size of the snake and the size of the cage, you want a design that will make cleaning easy. Additionally, your boa's cage would need to be capable of maintaining the right temperature.

For material, this would depend on the age of the snake. The younger boa constrictors are fine with paper towels or butcher paper, making the clean-up process easy.

However, for your older snake, we strongly recommend you cut up several pieces of indoor/outdoor carpeting. As they become soiled, they can be washed, 5% disinfectant then rinsed, dried, and reused.

Another option for your snake's cage is reptile bark. The only drawback here is that due to the sheer size of the cage and quantity of bark needed, it could get expensive. Make sure you avoid any type of wood shavings.

In addition to damaging the skin of the snake, this material could also be ingested, causing intestinal blockage or impaction. If you want to use reptile bark, feed the snake in a separate cage so it does not accidentally swallow the bark along with its food.

Furnishings

To help your boa constrictor feel more at home, safe, and secure, it will need places to hide. For this, we recommend you choose one close to the heat source and another on the other side of the cage where temperatures are cooler.

For this, use a half log, reptile cave, which is sold at pet stores and pet supply stores, upside down flowerpots, half of a coconut, or cardboard boxes. The challenge is that these should be larger than the snake.

Water

Your boa constrictor will need fresh water daily, as well as 50% humidity level, which can be reached by placing a large bowl of water in the cage with a heating element nearby to create the humidity.

With boas being so large and powerful, both the water dish and humidity dish will need to be sturdy.

Food

Generally, you want to feed your younger boa constrictor more often than you would an adult. For instance, the young snake should be fed about once a week, mid-age snakes being fed once every 10 to 14 days, and then mature snakes about every three weeks.

The goal here is to keep your snake healthy and strong so you may need to adjust the amount and frequency accordingly.

One of the common problems seen with boa constrictors kept in captivity is that people overfeed them, leading to a life of obesity. Therefore, while you want a well-rounded snake, you do not want one that is fat.

Meals for young boas should consist of mice, for mid-age snakes you want to feed rats, and for mature snakes, rabbits. In any case, make sure your snake is never fed food larger that the widest part of its body.

Then, you want to avoid handling your snake for 24 to 48 hours after eating to avoid regurgitation.

Boa constricts are different from other snakes when it comes to food. While you would feed many snakes dead food, because the boa constricts its food, the food should be live.

Now, keep in mind that some boas will accept killed food but not as often. Even then, the boa will likely wrap itself around the dead food, as if trying to suffocate it.

You will also find that boa constrictors disappear after eating. Do not be alarmed in that this is its natural response to eating.

Most importantly when feeding a boa is to use a separate cage for feeding. The reason is that the
59

boa would begin to associate your hand with food, which could mean a strike. However, because the boa is a rear-fanged snake, the bite would not be severe.

Boas also hunt their food in the wild by smell and sound. If you have handled food and then you go to stick your hand in the cage to feed your snake, it will smell and think your hand is prey. Instead, if you able, purchase an inexpensive handling stick, thus preventing the possibility of a bite.

Temperature

Since boa constrictors live in the tropical climates, they prefer warmer temperatures. Therefore, you want to keep the cage between 27.7(-32.2°C and 82-90°F during the day, nighttime temperatures 25.5-29.4°C and 78-85°F, and then it will need a basking spot that is between 32.2- 35°C and 90-95°F.

While food and water are important for keeping a boa constrictor, temperature is the most important element. To keep the temperatures this warm, you can use a combination of various heating elements, an under cage heater, incandescent bulbs, and so on.

As with all snakes, any heating device used should be placed outside the tank. This way, the snake cannot touch them, thus being burned. To create the basking spot, direct sun lighting or a heating element directly onto a rock but never use a hot rock.

Risks Associate with Boa Constrictors

Although a boa constrictor can make an excellent pet when handled properly and understood, we would be irresponsible if we did not inform you that there were risks associated with this type of snake. Boas have seriously injured and even killed children, household pets, and even adults so proper education and precautions are essential.

With a boa constrictor, the length of eight feet is considered a point of concern. This means the snake needs a large home and more than one person for handling.

Because of the potential risks of a large boa, we encourage you to be wise, only feeding it when someone else is around should something go awry.

While the Red Tailed Boa is smaller and considered a great pet for both beginner and advanced snake owners, it is still powerful. The Burmese Python (*Python molurus bivittatus*), which is a type of constrictor, is massive, strong, and can be dangerous.

Again snakes do not have to be feared but they should always be respected. They are wild animals, even if bred and raised in captivity. Therefore, if you are going to choose a boa, choose wisely.

Green Snake: *Opheodrys spp*

When it comes to the Green Snake, you will have your choice of two specific species that make great pets.

First, there is the Rough Green Snake: (*O. aestivus),* and second, the Smooth Green Snake: (*O. vernalis).*

The official names for these snakes translate to "summer tree serpent" and "spring tree serpent", respectively.

Regardless, both species of Green Snake are found in North America. For the

Rough species, they are more commonly found in some areas of Mexico and the eastern half of the United States while the Smooth species comes from the southern regions of Canada, as well as some parts of Texas.

On average, the Rough Green Snake reaches from 22 to 46 inches long whereas the Smooth Green Snake is much smaller, reaching lengths of 14 to 26 inches.

However, the female is most often larger and heavier than the male. These snakes are semi-arboreal, keeping low to the ground. Even so, the Rough species often spends time in the trees, vines, and bushes that overhang bodies of water since they are actually relatively good swimmers.

On the other hand, the Smooth species prefers meadows, fields, and grassy marshes, typically those along the edge of forests. As far as breeding, both species will mate in the spring with nesting from June to July.

However, the Green Snake will commonly go through a second breeding season. Females will lay the eggs in communal nests, as long as the nest is located in a great place.

On average, 2 to 14 eggs are laid and incubation of those eggs takes between 30 and 45 days for the Rough species and 4 to 23 days for the smooth species. However, if temperatures on cool, the eggs could take up to 80 days to hatch.

When baby Green Snakes are hatched, they are just about four to five inches in length but when full grown, they can reach up to 16 inches long. This particular snakes lives up to six years

Buying Tips

As with other snakes, you want to make sure the Green Snake you choose has healthy scales, alert eyes, are active and interested, its tongue flickers, and ask the seller about eating habits or any problems. You want to handle the snake so you can get a close-up look and feel.

Housing

Green snakes love vegetation such as what you would find in fields or gardens. Therefore, when preparing your Green Snake's cage, you want to make sure you keep this in mind.

Typically, a 30 gallon (113.5L) cage or aquarium will work quite well but since these snakes are so small and they enjoy exploration, make sure the cage has a locking lid with mesh top for air circulation.

In the cage, make sure there is green vegetation and overhanging branches, just as they would see in the wild. Placing small houseplants such as philodendrons in the cage is perfectly fine or you could use silk plants from your local hobby store.

When placing greenery in the cage, it should take up about one-third to one-half of the cage's space. Just make sure the vegetation is of different density and height.

Climbing

Green Snakes love to climb on live or silk plants. Therefore, make sure the cage offers both low-lying and higher plants.

Water

Fresh water needs to be provided to your Green Snake on a daily basis. In addition, many species of Green Snakes prefer to get their water from droplets found on leaves.

To accommodate this, keep live plants in the cage and mist them once or twice daily.

Food

The fascinating thing about Green Snakes is the diet, which consists of dragonflies, cockroaches, grasshoppers, butterfly caterpillars, land snails, fly larvae, and other similar things. Watching a Green Snake eat is quite interesting in that they are ferocious hunters, often catching their food in the air.

With keen eyesight, they have the ability to detect prey easily whereas most snakes use smell and vibration. When Green Snakes become overly excited, their skin will get a little bluish color to it, almost turquoise.

For some reason, the Green Snake is slow to accept food so if it does not eat right away, do not become alarmed.

You can encourage eating by offering a variety of food, all rich in nutrition. The only real consideration when feeding this species of snake is that you probably want to keep the number of mealworms to a limit to avoid the possible risk of impaction, instead focusing primarily on crickets.

Another consideration when feeding the Green Snake is that unlike other types of snakes, you should never offer food that is wider than its body. Then, to cut down on the chance of insects nibbling

65

on the snake, you should also provide food for the insects.

To store crickets and other food, keep them alive in Styrofoam containers with a lid that has air holes. Then at feeding time, place one or two crickets in a container, set on the floor of the cage, which will make it easier for the snake to find.

Temperature

Sometimes, a heat pad or UTH may be required to reach and maintain optimal temperature. For the Green Snake, you want the cage to stay between 23-26.6C (75 and 80F) during the day and then about 10 degrees cooler at night.

Just make sure you never place a glass cage in front of or too close to a window with direct sunlight, which could be deadly to this species. In fact, since the Green Snake is more active during the day (diurnal), we recommend you go with fluorescent lighting.

Rat Snake: *Elaphe obsoleta obsoleta*

The Rat Snake is a larger snake that comes from North America. While there are a number of species, the Black Rat Snake is a great choice that reaches to around five feet in length.

As the name suggests, the color is a deep black with patches of yellow, orange, red, or white between the scales. The underbelly of the Black Rat Snake is white or yellowish and near the head, you would notice a checkerboard type pattern.

The chin and throat area is a cream or white color and while young snakes begin gray with darker gray patches, as the Rat Snake grows, the adult coloration will begin to appear. Again, you will find many variations of the Rat Snake, to include those listed below:

Brindle

This is a distinct mutation where the entire body is covered with black speckles rather than the normal black coloring. With this, the blotches are quite clearly visible.

Red Albino

This amelanistic strain of the Black Rat Snake is created with red blotches on top of a white or cream-colored background.

White Albino

This amelanistic strain has cream or yellow blotches on a white background.

Buying Tips

A healthy Rat Snake should breathe normal and easy, be alert and active, curious about you just as much as you are about it, have clear eyes, and move about freely. Check the top and underside of the snake as well for any sores or open wounds that could be a problem for infection, along with signs of parasites.

Housing

The adult Rat Snake will need a minimum of a 113.5L (30-gallon) tank although we actually recommend larger. Be sure you choose a lid that can be secured down since Rat Snakes are notorious escapers.

As far as bedding material, you can keep it simple with a Rat Snake. For instance, shredded up newspaper, paper towels, aspen wood shavings, cypress mulch, and other similar substrate are great choices. The only thing to remember is that cedar or pine shavings should never be used since they contain toxic chemicals that can cause illness or injury to the snake.

Furnishings

The Rat Snake needs several places to hide so you want to provide many different hide boxes. The key here is to choose one that is large enough for the snake to enter after eating, another that is just slightly tighter, giving the snake more security, and third containing sphagnum moss that can be misted to provide needed humidity. Just be sure not to get the moss too wet.

Climbing

Your Rat Snake will need a couple of branches to climb since this is a favorite pastime. Just to make sure the branch or branches are sturdy to hold the snake's weight. If you find a stick in the backyard, you can prepare it for the snake by removing the bark and then baking it at 180° C (350° F) for one hour to help remove any parasites and microbes. You might also consider adding a larger rock or raised platform for climbing.

Water

The Rat Snake will need fresh water daily, in a dish large enough for it to slither through at will.

Food

Typically, the black Rat Snake will feed regular, pre-killed mice and rats. For baby snakes, start them out on pinkies, feeding every four to six days. Once the snake matures, you can switch to regular mice and rats, changing the feed schedule to seven to ten days. Just make sure the size of the food is no larger than the greatest width of the snake.

Temperature

The Rat Snake's cage needs to be a temperature gradient so the snake can regulate its body moving from cool end to warm end and vise versa. An excellent way to achieve this is with an under tank heater.

69

Then, you want to create optimal temperature for this snake between 27.7 C and 29.4C (82 and 85F). However, you want the cool side of the cage to be around 21.1C (70F)

Lighting

The Rat Snake does not have any specific lighting requirements. On the other hand, if you want to illuminate the cage for your own viewing pleasure, we suggest fluorescent lighting.

Other Possible Choices

In addition to the species of snakes provided above, the following are some other species that you might consider.

Hognose Snake: *Heterodon sp.*

Commonly seen in captivity by snake enthusiasts, the Hognose Snakes come in a number of subspecies. The fun thing about this species is the distinct look and coloration. For instance, males have 35 dorsal blotches whereas the female has 40.

Then, you will see an albino morph version of the Hognose Snake, which are yellow with bright orange blotches or axanthics, which are silver with gray to black blotches, both that are beautiful.

Rubber Boa: *Thamnophis spp.*

This particular Boa Constrictor is a nice size, reaching lengths between 14 and 33 inches.

When kept in captivity, you would need to make sure the cage has adequate humidity since this snake comes from damp woodlands and coniferous forests.

Milk Snake: *Lampropeltis triangulum*

See more often on the East Coast, the Milk Snake can grow quite long, more than six feet in some cases. This particular snake looks similar to the Coral Snake with the exception that the bands are red and black.

As they say in the jungle to tell the two snakes apart – "red and black, friend of Jack – red and yellow, kill a fellow".

Rose Boa Constrictor: *Lichanura trivigata*

This Boa is a great addition as a pet. Reaching between 24 and 42 inches long, the Rosy Boa comes from warmer climates of South and North California as well as Southwest Arizona. This snake enjoys a warm cage but also moisture.

Bull Snake: *Pituophis spp.*

The Bull Snake is found throughout the United States. This large, stock snake can reach between five and six feet in length and has a massive girth.

Although the Bull Snake is not the most colorful species, it is a great snake to keep. Just be sure you have the right size cage to accommodate its large size.

Gopher Snake: *Pituophis catenifer*

Located throughout the United States, the Gopher Snake can be mistaken for a Rattlesnake when cornered but when handled properly, they can be good pets for experienced snake handlers.

General Information about Snakes

While different breeds of snakes have different requirements in some areas, snakes also share things. In this chapter, we wanted to talk about some of the generalities seen from one snake breed to another.

Determining Gender

If you are curious whether you have a boy or girl Corn Snake, you can sex them to determine the gender but be aware, the process is somewhat challenging. Unlike other snakes, the Corn Snake does not display different color between male and female nor do they differ much in size.

Making the gender identification even more challenging is the fact that there is no obvious external genitalia and behavior between male and female is much the same.

Popping

The technique called "popping" can be used but we strongly suggest you have your snake examined by a professional snake handler, breeder, or veterinarian who can perform this technique the right way.

Regardless, this involves looking at the physical aspects of the snake. You see male snakes have two penises or a forked penis.

These internal organs will pop out during breeding season through the vent, which is a small slip on the underside of the snake. The size of the vent can be small or take up as much as 80% of the underside of the belly.

Only young snakes can be tested with the popping technique since pressure is applied to the vent, causing the penis or hemipenes to pop out but if not done right, damage to the organ can occur, which is why only a professional should do this.

Probing

For probing, this technique can be done at any age, although it is usually done only on older snakes after a time when popping is not longer practical or effective.

For this technique, the expert would use an actual probing apparatus, which is then inserted into the vent.

Depending on how far into the vent the probe goes would determine male from female Again, while not an unpleasant experience for the snake, if not done properly, it could cause damage.

External Examination

This technique is one you could do yourself. Although not 100% science, it would give you a good idea as to the snake's gender. Start by looking around the tail section, going from the vent to the thickest part of the snake.

If you notice any bulging, it could be a male due to the penis. In addition, the male Corn Snake will usually have a tail slightly longer and broader than the female.

Then, the male snake will often have an overall appearance that is thinner than the female.

Handling Your Snake

For even-tempered snakes such as the Corn or King Snake, both adults and kids alike can handle them with ease. However, learning to handle your new snake can be a little bit daunting.

Just remember, docile snakes will not bite you. Therefore, be confident and everything will work out great. Even if this breed of snake were to bite, you would feel nothing because they have such small teeth.

The most important aspect of holding and handling your snake is to create trust. To do this, you should handle it when young and then several times a week. The process is simple but takes a little time.

First, allow your snake time to settle into the new home, becoming familiar and comfortable with the new surroundings. Then, slowly reach your hand into the cage, rubbing the back of its head and body gently and slowly.

Do this several times a day for about a week or two so your snake becomes accustomed to your hand and touch. If your snake should try to slither away, do not grab it or hold it back.

Instead, just let it have its freedom to move at will. In a few weeks, your snake will understand that your hand feeds it, waters it, cleans its cage, and is gentle – thus the trust.

Make sure your hands are warm and then gently reach your hand underneath the part of its body near the head to pick it up. If it is grown, then use your other hand to provide support on the back end of the body.

Snakes love to have the skin underneath the chin rubbed so if it appears a little worried, start petting him. Some snakes will actually start to fall asleep.

Again, be confident, knowing this snake is not going to harm you. Typically, 10 to 15 minutes of handling at a time is adequate for both you and the snake. When first starting out, we recommend you hold the snake over a bed, rug, or get down close to the ground. With this, should the snake wiggle and scare you, with accidentally dropping it, there would be no injury.

In addition, hold your snake in close proximity of the cage, just in case it becomes too squirmy you can simply place it back inside. Then, never hold your snake outside since most love to explore and they are great escape artists.

Therefore, were to get away, you would probably never find it again variations but when it comes to breeding, you can mix and match anyway you want.

Snakes usually breed better in the springtime. Remember, when holding your snake, it will likely want to slither through your fingers and even around your arm and neck.

Allow the snake time to do this which for it, is fun. Unfortunately snakes will sometimes defecate while being held so if this happens take care not to drop the snake.

Simply place it back in the cage and clean up! If you have a snake that requires a little more attention or support, you should work with a friend or another snake enthusiast to make sure your snake is handled properly.

If the snake bites, you would need to handle it different from a docile snake. In this case, the key is to get the head pressed firmly but gently against the bottom of the cage. For this, you could use a special stick like device sold at pet stores.

With the head securely down, slowly reach your hand behind its head, grabbing it on either side and just above where the opening is.

You do not want to squeeze so hard that you do harm but firm enough that the snake cannot turn to bite. With this position, the snake's mouth is always in front of the hand, unable to reach you.

If the snake should try to wiggle around using its body, just keep hold of the head without letting go. This obviously takes practice and is not intended for the inexperienced.

Breeding Snakes

If you want to breed your snake, good news, you can. Of all snakes kept in captivity, the Corn Snake is the easiest but most snakes can be bred with absolute success.

The best age for breeding your snake is from 18 to 24 months but only if healthy and well fed. Keep in mind that snakes come in different color and pattern.

In fact, after placing a male and female together, you will actually notice them flirting with each other.

As you will discover in our **Bonus Book**, ***"Successful Snake Breeding"***, you can enjoy little baby snakes of your own, either for the sheer enjoyment of it or to sell.

Health and Wellness of Your Snake

Just as with any type of pet, snakes get sick and experience injury. This chapter provides valuable information on the types of things your snake may face, along with tips of things you can do to keep the snake healthy.

Sometimes, you have several options to help your snake through a difficult time but keep in mind that you might need to have your snake checked by a veterinarian, one that understands that special needs of snakes.

The following are a few of the common things you might experience when owning a snake. However, for a more complete list, you will find tons of information in **Bonus Book**: ***"Keeping your Snake Healthy"***.

With the information provided in the bonus book, you can use it as a reference so you know what to look for, what causes the problem, and what to do to get your snake healthy again.

Constipation

Symptoms

Not defecating

Causes

Illness
Dehydration
Injury
Parasite infestation
Cloacoliths
Environmental temperature (not optimal)

Solution

Constipation among snakes kept in captivity is common. One of the best solutions is to fill your sink or a separate aquarium with very warm but not hot water, allowing the snake to "soak" in the water for about 25 to 30 minutes.

Try this for a couple of times a day for three to four days. If you do not get results, then your snake should be seen by a veterinarian.

Fungal Infection

Symptoms

Signs of skin or eye infection to include redness, swelling, open sores, pus, etc.

Causes

Damp, dirty cages
80

Solution

If your snake shows signs of a fungal infection, you want it to be treated by a veterinarian. Keep in mind that some types of fungal infection such as ringworm are contagious to both humans and other family pets.

Therefore, if ringworm were the problem, the snake and other affected people/pets would need to be treated. Typically, a topical and systemic ointment will work fine but in severe cases, a veterinarian will inject antibiotics.

Abnormal Shedding

Symptoms

Snake begins to shed but the process stops Retained eye caps (white/gray covering during the shedding process)

Causes

Previous injury to scales
Lack of hard surfaces on which the snake can rub
Inadequate humidity levels
Internal disease
External parasites
Thyroid gland problems

Solution

If your snake has stopped shedding in the middle of the process, you need to seek veterinarian care immediately.

Typically, the veterinarian will soak the snake in warm water for a few hours, after which time a damp towel would be used to peel the remaining skin off gently.

Although this sounds like an easy process, it should only be done by a professional in that doing it wrong could result in serious injury.

As far as Retained Eye Caps, this too is related to an abnormal shedding process. The snake's eye caps are comprised of the outer cellular layer of the cornea.

When the snake sheds, this would normally shed as well. However, if the snake goes through an abnormal shed, both the skin and eye do not shed as they should.

You can talk to your veterinarian about using softening ointments but if this does not work, the veterinarian would need to remove the corneal remnants, something that should never be tried at home.

Scale Rot

Symptoms

Discolored ventral scales, usually red, brown, or pink

Chipped ventral scales

Causes

Internal infection that works its way to the outside skin (caused by dried feces and urates left in the cage)

Solution

The best treatment for Scale Rot is to use an antibiotic cream such as Neosporin on the affected area. In addition, make sure the snake's cage is clean and sanitized.

Keep in mind that you will probably not see much change until the snake sheds its skin. This type of irritation will naturally start the shedding cycle most of the time.

Now, after cleaning your snake's cage, we recommend you leave out the bedding material while applying the antibiotic cream twice daily.

If you notice redness spreading or the infection becoming worse, the infection could be septic or in the blood at which time it could spread quickly to vital organs, killing the snake.

Therefore, the veterinarian would need to administer serious antibiotics to stop the infection.

Equipment and Accessories

As discussed earlier, the size of your snake's cage will depend largely on size and habitat requirements. However, this chapter will focus on your options for cages along with other accessories you might consider buying.

In addition, we will provide you some great resources where everything you need for your snake can be purchased.

Housing

Because snakes have limited activity, you do not need to go out and buy a huge cage. However, you want the size of the cage to be large enough so your snake can move about and explore.

Therefore, when choosing your snake's cage, remember it will grow into a mature snake needing more room than when it was young.

Now, when thinking about space, you need to keep both horizontal and vertical space in mind since many snakes love to climb. The most affordable and efficient type cage is a standard Plexiglas or glass aquarium, the kind you would use for fish.

In addition to providing the snake with a secure home, it also provides you with ample viewing area so you can enjoy the snake to the fullest.

This type of cage has yet another benefit in that it is ideal for maintaining the perfect temperature and humidity level needed for your snake to live. Plexiglas or glass cages also make breeze.

Cage Size

To provide you with some guidelines as to the exact size, use the following:

Length – The tank should be two-thirds of the snake's body length

Width – The tank should be one-half of the snake's body length

Small Snakes – The tank should be two feet long or less (Garter Snake)

Medium Snakes – The tank should be between 20 and 30 gallons

(Corn Snakes, Milk Snake, etc)

Large Snakes – The tank should be 55 gallons and up (Boa Constrictors and larger Boids)

Now, regardless of the type or size of the snake, if you have a species that is active, then you would go up in size. Additionally, if your snake loves to climb or needs dense vegetation such as the Green Snake, again, go with a larger cage to accommodate the other features within the cage.

Finally, if you purchase a baby snake, remember it will grow so when buying the cage, choose for the snake's full size.

Secured Lid

The one thing to remember however is that you need a good, locking lid with wire mesh so your snake will have adequate fresh air while still being in an enclosed and protected environment.

This will eliminate your snake from escaping while also providing it with a safe enclosure to dissuade injuries to the nose and/or surrounding tissue while trying to escape.

Then be sure the lid has a clamp or lock for two reasons. First, snakes are powerful creatures, able to use their noses to push lids open.

Second, this will keep small children or other people out of the cage who should not be handling the snake.

The bottom line is that the size of the cage really depends on the mature size and activity level of the snake, as well as the number of snakes you keep in one cage.

Temperature

Snakes are cold-blooded creatures. Since they are not capable of creating their own body heat, they need proper temperature in the cage.

Therefore, for the health and happiness of your snake, the cage must be maintained at the optimal temperature for the species you own.

If the temperature is not correct, the snake will not be able to digest its food, its activity level will be decreased, the snake will have a lower defense to disease, and so on.

The key to success it to establish a temperature gradient, meaning you would need to determine the right temperature for your type of snake. As an example, many snakes such as Garter Snakes and Rat Snakes do well with temperatures ranging from the 70s to 80s (23-26C) during the warmer daytime hours and then 60 to 70 degrees(15.5C to21C) at night.

One of the most important things is that after your snake has been fed, the temperature in the cage should be at the highest possible setting for the particular species to help with digestion.

You have a number of methods for increasing the heat of the cage but as mentioned – NO HOT ROCKS! Instead, some of the best options include the following:

Heat Tape

For substrate heat, this is an excellent solution. Heat tape is versatile and designed for inside or outside of the cage use. With this, you will need to use a thermostat so you have the exact temperature being maintained.

There is some wiring involved but the process is easy. Keep in mind that to avoid electrical shock when using on the inside of the cage, you will need to make sure the contacts are well insulated but also protected from water and moisture.

Heat Pad

When buying a heat pad for your snake's cage, you can choose from the adhesive style or the under tank heater (UTH).

These both work very well for aquariums but again, it is essential you use a thermostat along with the heater so you maintain optimal heat.

Heat Lamp

For arboreal species of snakes, heat lamps work best. Used for basking, you can place a flat rock in the cage with the heat lamp beaming down. With this, the snake will come out into the open to enjoy the heat.

Ceramic Heat

Ceramic heaters are also a good option for keeping snakes warm. These **"light bulbs"** just screw into a standard light socket but provide only heat, no light. If you use a ceramic heater, you would also want to make sure your snake gets about 12 hours of light. However many snakes have been burnt by these heat lamps so ensure you snake doesn't have access to coil around or touch the lamp.

Radiant Heat Panels

Although more expensive than other types of heaters, radiant heat panels are actually more economical long-term. While you could use this type of heat for all species of snakes, it does exceptionally well for larger species.

Heat Rocks

Yes – we keep talking about heat or hot rocks but it is so important you NOT use one for your snake. Although advertised as being safe, far too many snakes have experienced serious burns due to hot spots. While some people swear by them, we suggest you avoid the potential for harm.

Lighting

You want to make sure that your snake cycles light and dark, which means having it on 12 hours and then off 12 hours. Most snakes do very well with supplemental lighting, since they spend a good part of their life in hiding. The following are options you might consider:

Incandescent

Incandescent lighting works quite well but keep in mind that this lighting also gets very hot. Now, if you want to create warmth on a rock where your snake can bask, then incandescent lighting is a great solution.

However, the most important thing is to protect the snake from coming into contact with the light or it would likely experience serious burn. Therefore, make sure this type of lighting is always kept on the outside of the cage.

Fluorescent

The great thing about fluorescent lighting is a great choice in that you get the light while not having to worry about excessive heat. You can choose from various shapes and sizes. Best of all, fluorescent lighting is affordable to buy and to operate.

Humidity

Another important aspect of maintaining a good environment for your snake is the humidity. If the cage does not have enough humidity, then the snake could experience dehydration along with other problems, specifically when shedding.

On the other hand, if the cage has too high humidity, the snake might experience things such as respiratory infection, blisters, and so on.

Just as with food, cage size, and heat, different species of snakes need different levels of humidity. For starters, make sure the snake always has fresh water, which is for both drinking along with soaking.

If you need additional moisture, place a second dish of water directly under the light source. You could also add live plants and mist them about once a week. If you are uncertain that the levels are where they should be, you can purchase a humidity meter.

You might make a humidity box, which is specifically designed for snakes going through the shedding phase.

For this, place a moist paper towel or sorghum moss into a small plastic container with holes poked in the lid.

Something as simple as a small, empty, and clean butter container works well. The goal is that while shedding, humidity in the cage should be maintained at 60%.

Bedding Material

Again, you can use things for your snake's bedding that you already have around the home or purchase special type bedding.

For instance, shredded newspaper, paper towels, and indoor/outdoor carpeting are all excellent options.

In the case of the newspaper and paper towel, when the cage becomes dirty, you simply throw it out and replace it with new.

In the case of the indoor/outdoor carpeting, you can wash this off, allow it to dry, and then place it back inside the cage, which is a great money-saver.

Things to Avoid

Certain materials could prove dangerous to your pet, causing penetration injury to the body or from ingestion. These include:

Pea gravel
Crushed corncob
Kitty liter
Wood shavings (different from wood chips)
Cedar of any kind

Although these types of bedding material look nice, they are a definite no-no.

What happens is that these materials can trap in moisture and feces, which becomes a breeding ground for bacteria, ultimately leading to infection or parasites.

Then, as the snake slithers through the bedding after its prey, it could easily swallow some of it causing all types of problems to include obstruction of the digestive tract.

Environmental Features

Since snakes love and need to climb and hide, it is important that you create an environment that is similar to its natural habitat.

Tree Branches & Ropes

You could literally walk through your backyard, looking for an appropriate size branch to leave against the side of the cage, which would be ideal for climbing. Another great option is a hanging rope, which can be made or purchased.

Vegetation

Then, you might consider vegetation, which could be in the form of live or silk plants. While some snakes are not as concerned with vegetation, others such as the Green Snake need vegetation to survive.

Hiding

Most snakes need privacy. In fact, you will find that many species of snakes will not eat until they have a hidden place to take the prey.

An empty paper towel holder is a great option but you can also purchase a hiding box, which is designed specifically for snakes in captivity.

Just remember that whatever you put in the cage should be large enough to accommodate not only your snake's body but also its growing body or a body full of food.

Australian Poisonous Snakes

Australia houses some of the most venomous snakes in the world and there certainly are a few of them. There are four rear-fanged venomous species and 53 front-fanged. Even though many of our snakes are venomous only 15 species can inject a fatal bite. Antivenin is readily available.

Rear fanged snakes

Brown tree snake *Boiga irregulari*
Bockadam   *Cerberus australis*
White Bellied Mangrove Snake *Fordonia leucobalia*
Richardson Mangrove Snake *Myron richardsonii*

Front fanged Snakes

Common Death Adder *Acanthophis antarcticus*
Northern Death Adder *Acanthophis praelongus*
Blacksoil *Death Adder Acanthophis hawkei*
Highlands Copperhead *Austrelaps ramsayi*
Australian Coral Snake *Brachyurophis australi*
Narrow Banded Shovel Nosed *Snake Brachyurophis fasciolatu*
Unbanded Shovel Nosed *Snake Brachyurophis*

incinctus
Northern Shovel Nosed Snake *Brachyurophis roperi*
Southern Shoveled Nosed Snake *Brachyurophis
semifasciatus*
Northern Dwarf Crowned *Snake Cacophis Churchill*
White crowned Snake *Cacophis harriettae*
Golden Crowned Snake *Cacophis squamulosus*
Krefft's Dwarf Snake *Cacophis krefftii*
Carpentaria Snake *Cryptophis boschmai*
Black striped Snake *Cryptophis nigrostriatus*
Small Eyed Snake *Cryptophis nigrescens*
Secretive Snake *Cryptophis pallidiceps*
Yellow Faced Whip Snake *Demania psammophis*
Collared Whip Snake *Demansia torquata*
Grey Whip Snake *Demansia simplex*
Lesser Black Whip Snake *Demansia vestigata*
Devils' BandedSnake *Densonia devisi*
Ornamental Snake *Densonia maculate*
White Lipped Snake *Drysdalia coronoides*
Blue Mountains Crowned Snake *Drysdalia
rhodogaster*
Moon Snake *Furina ornate*
Red Naped Snake *Furina diadema*
Grey Snake *Hemiaspis damelii*
Marsh Snake *Hemiaspis signata*
Paled Headed Snake *Hopocephalus* bitorquatus
Broad Headed *Snake Hopocephalus bungaroides*
Stephen's Banded Snake *Hopocephalus stephensi*
Tiger Snake *Notechis scutanus Can Be Fatal*
Western Taipan *Oxyuranus microlepidotus Can Be
Fatal*
Coastal Taipan *Oxyuranus scutellatus Can Be Fatal*

Dwyer's Snake *Parasuta dwyeri*
Little Whip Snake *Parasuta flagellum*
Spectacled Snake *Parasuta specabillus*
King Brown Snake *Pseudechis australis Can Be Fatal*
Collett's Snake *Pseudechis colletti Can Be Fatal*
Red-Bellied Black Snake *Pseudechis porphyriacus Can Be Fatal*
Spotted Black Snake *Pseudechis guttatus Can Be Fatal*
Ringed Brown Snake *Pseudechis modesta*
Western Brown Snake *Pseudechis nuchalis*
Eastern Brown Snake *Pseudechis textilis*
Speckled Brown Snake *Pseudechis guttata*
West Coast Banded Snake *Simoselaps littoralis*
Myall Snake *Suta suta*
Rough Scaled Snake *Tropidechis carinatus*
Eastern Bandy Bandy *Vermicella annulata*
Northern Bandy Bandy *Vermicella intermedia*
Narrow Banded Bandy Bandy *Vermicella multifasciata*

To check out Australia's most venomous snake Listing see

http://www.avru.org/general/general mostvenom.html.

Eastern Brown Snake

5th most Venomous in the world

Eastern Brown, strike distance is whole body length, from any direction 360degrees. Flexible head to squeeze into narrow spaces after mice, coils up to strike, strikes with its mouth open for maximum damage.

Interesting Fact: One of only two species which are able to see directly with their eyes. All other snakes besides the Eastern Brown and Copperhead have to turn their heads slightly to the side as their eyes are more positioned like birds.

U.S. Poisonous Snakes

When it comes to poisonous snakes in the United States, most cannot be kept in captivity and for those that are a special permit must be obtained.

While you would now own a poisonous snake as a pet, we wanted to provide you with a list of some considered "non-captive". The list would be much too great to put in one book but the following will give you an idea of rattlesnakes.

Rattlesnakes

Especially in warm climate regions such as California and Arizona, Rattlesnakes are common. In all, there are 16 unique varieties of Rattlesnakes, which come in various color combinations and subspecies.

However, the one common denominator is the rattle on the tip of the tail that when threatened or frightened, will be raised in the air and rattled to warn approaching predators to stay away.

Black-Tailed Rattlesnake
Canebrake Rattlesnake
Eastern Diamondback Rattlesnake

Massasauga Rattlesnake
Mojave Rattlesnake
Pacific Rattlesnake
Pigmy Rattlesnake
Prairie Rattlesnake
Sidewinder
Speckled Rattlesnake
Timber Rattlesnake
Western Diamondback Rattlesnake

Interestingly, Rattlesnakes seldom grow to more than two feet long. However, you will discover a few species that can grow to six or seven feet.

On the end of the tail is a rattle. In addition, the Rattlesnake possesses a facial pit between the eye and nose. Depending on the species, some have small scales on the top of the head as well while others have large scales.

In addition, Rattlesnakes have very small, beady eyes, with elliptical pupils. Keep in mind that a bite from a Rattlesnake can be not only dangerous but also deadly. The venom injected into the skin is painful and damaging to tissue and nerves.

Of all Rattlesnake species is the Mojave Rattlesnake! As you will see from the information below, we have chosen a few of these species to summarize.

Canebrake Rattlesnake

This species is also called the Timber Rattlesnake.

The color of the skin allows the snake to blend in with shadows and leaves, perfect for spying on prey.

This particular Rattlesnake can reach between four and five feet and found primarily in swamps.

Eastern Diamond Back Rattlesnake

This is one of the largest Rattlesnakes, easily reaching between six and seven feet in length.

The diamond pattern on the back is where the name comes from, which extend the entire length of the snake's body.

This type of Rattlesnake likes living in flat woods or sand hills in grassy areas near salt marshes, close to the coast, and in open areas and oak-palmetto hammocks.

Pigmy Rattlesnake

Of all Rattlesnake species, this is the smallest, thus the name.

Reaching just one to two feet, this snake prefers pine flat woods and grassy areas.

Because the rattle on this snake is so small, it sounds more like a cricket than a rattle.

Other Poisonous Snakes

In addition to Rattlesnakes, there are many other poisonous snakes in the United

States but interestingly, just four can kill.

These include the Coral Snake, Copperhead, Cottonmouth, Water Moccasin and the Rattlesnake.

Coral Snake

This poisonous snake is extremely toxic and resembles several nonpoisonous snakes, which is why knowledge is very important.

Although the Coral Snake does not have fangs, has a small mouth and little teeth, biting on a person's fingers and toes is the primary target.

In addition, the Coral Snake will chew on the skin while the poison is being injected. The skin of the Coral Snake is actually very beautiful with red, yellow, and black coloration.

The venom of this snake is neurotoxin, which means it paralyzes the nerves.

Unfortunately, the fatality rate of bites from Coral Snakes is high but if treated within two hours, there is a chance of recovery.

Copperhead

The Copperhead has the ability to blend in with the environment easily, just waiting for prey. Growing from two to three feet in length Copperheads usually live in overgrown or in swampy areas.

The young have sulfur/yellow tipped tails and while the adult bite is venomous, the younger snake has an even more deadly bite.

Although the toxic of a Copperhead is considered mild, fatalities have been reported.

The young have sulfur/yellow tipped tails and while the adult bite is venomous, the younger snake has an even more deadly bite.

Although the toxic of a Copperhead is considered mild, fatalities have been reported

Cottonmouth Water Moccasin

Related to the Copperhead, the Cottonmouth is far more dangerous. The venom of this snake is highly toxic causing severe destruction of the tissue.

Young and mature Cottonmouth can be distinguished easily. Growing from three to six feet in length, the Cottonmouth is not a snake to recon with and if bitten, immediate emergency care is required.

Understanding Venom

First – not all snakes are venomous. In fact, with more than 2,700 species of snakes, only 300 are venomous!

Although you would likely not own a venomous snake, we wanted to provide you with some interesting facts just for fun!

Interesting Facts

Venom is made and then stored in glands located behind and below the snake's eyes

Small ducts or passageways move the venom to the hollow fangs of the snake

Venom originates from the digestive enzymes located in the stomach

The venom is a unique mixture of enzymes and proteins. In fact, there are approximately 20 different toxic enzymes in poisons. While no one venomous snake has all of these enzymes, most have between 6 and 12.

Keep in mind that each enzyme has a unique function, as shown here:

Adenosine Triphosphatase – Believed to be one of the primary agents that causes shock while immobilizing prey.

Amino Acid Oxidase – Helps with digestion and triggering of other enzymes, while giving venom its yellowish coloring

Cholinesterase – Attacks the nervous system, relaxing the body's muscles so much that the person or animal bitten has zero control

Hyaluronidase – Causes other enzymes to be absorbed quicker

Phosphodiesterase – Accounts for the negative cardiac reaction seen in victims, specific to a serious drop in blood pressure

Proteinase – Plays a major role in the digestive process, breaking down tissue at a fast rate

Once bitten, snake venom immobilizes the victim or prey by attacking the central nervous system while venom travels through the muscular and blood systems of the body.

To avoid being bitten by a snake, when in the wild or areas known for poisonous snakes, where high top, thick leather boots and long pants.

Venom is used as a means of defense and protection.

Venomous snakes are **"squamates"**.

Types of Venom

When talking about snake venom, it is divided into two primary categories.

108

First is the hemotoxicity category and second, the neurotoxicity category.

Hemotoxicity – This type of snake venom affects **organs and the blood**.

With this, you would see inflammation, swelling, or breakdown within the body. Of all types of snakebites, the hemotoxic is by far the most excruciating, specifically as tissue dies and breathing becomes difficult.

Neurotoxic – With this type of snakebite, the **nervous system** is involved, which means the person or prey would likely experience seizures and possible death. While hemotoxic bites hurt, neurotoxin bites are the most deadly.

Fascinating Questions

Over time, we have gathered questions from people from around the country interesting in learning all they can about owning snakes and snakes in general. We wanted to dedicate this chapter to addressing some of the fascinating questions that do not necessarily fall within other categories.

The Escape Artist

As a snake owner, there will probably be more than one time when you go to see your pet only to discover it has taken itself for a walk – outside of the cage. This occurrence is relatively common and nothing to fear. The challenge comes in finding your snake so it can be returned home safely.

We recommend you start searching around the cage, specifically in the room where the cage is located. Pay attention to baseboard areas, window seals, under furniture, and anything that the snake could use for climbing. For instance, if you have an artificial tree, check it or if you have a rope plant holder, follow it to the top.

If the snake is not anywhere obvious, you want to start your search in cabinets, drawers, behind books in bookshelves, on shelves, literally any place where a snake could hide.

Check under couch and chair cushions, under the mattresses, behind window treatments, and if the toilet lid is up, even in the toilet. Other places such as:

Kleenex boxes, purses, backpacks, shoes, or any other dark, hiding place is a possibility.

With a loose snake in the house, leave no stone unturned. If you have checked behind all of the appliances, in dressers, laundry baskets, and throughout the house but without success, you would now need to try some things to lure it back home.

The most important thing is that during the time the snake is still out make sure any doors or windows leading to the outside are shut.

In addition, if you have a basement, after checking it thoroughly, close the door, which will narrow down the possibilities of where the snake can go. Now, to entice the snake to return home, keep the door opened wide so if it wants to slither back in, there is no problem. Additionally, place some of the snake's favorites treats inside the cage.

For instance, if your snake loves live crickets, then put some in a box so the snake can smell them. Then, place some tin foil on the floor leading to the cage so you would be able to hear the return.

If all else fails, sprinkle a little bit of white flour on the floor in areas where you think the snake might have gone. If it travels through that way, you would be able to follow the powdery trail.

Just remember, even large snakes are capable of getting into very small places so you will need to check everything. In addition, many snakes are nocturnal, meaning they are most active at night. In this case, leave just a small night light on and wait for the snake to makes its way back to the cage.

Snakes are very much aware that the cage is its home. Therefore, place the cage on the floor where the snake can reach it should it come back. Finally, if your snake has been out longer than 12 hours, be sure you place a water dish on the floor as well.

Snakes and Medicine

Various parts of snakes have been used in Chinese medicine dating back to recorded times of 100 AD. For example, sloughed snakeskin was used as a treatment for superficial disease such as open wounds, opacities, sore throat, eye infection, and even hemorrhoids.

Additionally, the gallbladder of the snake was used according to historians starting around 520 AD along with the meat of a pit viper and the skin for treating various types of skin disease, hemorrhage, and chronic pain.

Other recordings from 600 AD show that both the white-patterned pit viper and non-toxic black-striped snake were used specifically for food and health.

However, the most famous Chinese era was during the Tang Dynasty in which many different medicines were used from snakes. When it comes to traditional healers, three main parts of the snake are considered relative to medicine and healing.

For example, a snake is highly flexible, which means people living with stiffness would benefit. In fact, in today's society, you will find both the Zaocys and

Agkistrodon snakes used specifically for treating people with arthritis.

Then, snakes are fast. With this, it is believed substances made from snake in use for healing would work quickly within the body. Finally, snakes shed their skin, meaning people would see regeneration benefits from the snake.

With this belief, many parts of the snake are used. Using sloughed skin, you can now find a number of ointments on the market formulated for people with psoriasis, acne, rash, itching skin, etc.

Snakeskin has and continues to be considered an excellent solution for treating the cornea of the eye by reducing cloudiness that you would see with cataracts and other forms of disease. Interestingly, venom of snakes is also currently used as antivenin for people bitten, as well as the treatment of such things as convulsions.

You will also discover snake bile a valued tonic used as a health drink in many Asian restaurants. This "drink" is said to have a sweet aftertaste that helps stimulate the appetite, treat whooping cough, high fever, and hemorrhoids, bleeding of the gums, rheumatic pain, convulsions, skin infections, and more.

However, one of the most popular of all snake remedies is the mixture of three gallbladders with an herb called fritillaria. Made into a powder or in liquid form, this

Chinese concoction is believed to help with many things, specifically cough and bronchitis.

We also see snakes now being used in the treatment of some forms of cancer, specifically leukemia. For this, a powder is made from the water snake. In addition, venom has now shown value in the treatment of cardiovascular disease and high blood pressure. Today, the use of snakes is seen primarily in Asian countries but there is a small market in the United States.

With the gallbladder of the snake being the most valued part of the body, some concern has been raised as far as shortage. In fact, literally tons of snakes used for medicine in China alone are in the tons. While this remains somewhat controversial for westernized countries, some people are beginning to see the benefit as they try powdered forms and then see results.

Snakebites

Sometimes, snakebites are so minor and insignificant that you would not even know you had been bitten. However, other bits could be deadly, such as those from venomous snakes.

Take the Garter and Corn Snakes for example. These snakes are small with tiny teeth. Therefore, should you be bitten, chances are you would not even notice.

Other snakes kept in captivity can bite but typically, this would be due to feeling threatened or scared or the smell of mice may still be on the lingering on the feeders hand. For non-venomous snakes, if you should be bitten, you want to wash the wound thoroughly under clean, running water.

Then, sterilize the area with disinfectant. If the bite is bleeding and not stopping when pressure is applied, you might need to visit the doctor to have a few stitches but in most cases, this would be rare.

Keep in mind that if you have a large snake and the bite was bad, then you might have a problem with blood loss. In this case, too much blood loss could result in shock. If the blood loss is substantial, even death could occur.

When someone goes into shock, the skin will become pale, cold and clammy, the individual may feel disoriented, and feel dizzy. You can find more on shock in the First Aid Chapter below here.

If you have this type of snakebite, then you need to be kept warm, raising the legs about 8 to 10 inches to help with blood flow to the brain. This also helps any possibility with collapse.

Now, if this should happen with a captive snake, your chances of getting help are as easy as dialing Triple Zero **000 or 112** for mobile phones within Australia or **911** in USA.

However, if you were to experience a bad snakebite in the wild, then you need to take special care specific to the type of species. **ALWAYS assume the bite has been inflicted by a venomous snake in the wild.**

If the snake were non-venomous, then you could take your time getting help from the nearest medical facility. On the other hand, if you were bitten by a venomous snake, then you should try to identify the species.

Do not try to kill or capture the snake fore in fact that is when most bites will occur. Get to the hospital immediately, without wasting any time.

The goal is to remain calm to keep your metabolism down. If your metabolism speeds up, the venom would move through the body faster.

On the other hand, if a venomous snake bit you, get to the hospital immediately, without wasting time. As mentioned previously remain calm and still as to not increase the venom spreading through your body faster.

Do not try to capture the snake as snakebites generally happen to those whom attempt to capture or kill a wild snake. Besides this, use of your muscles will help the venom travel quicker around your body.

Take notice of the area you are in, swampy wetland, dry grassland etc for identifying a snake by describing colouring or markings may prove quite difficult as their markings and colour differ within all species for example, a Tiger Snake may not have any bandings on it skin.

Snake Bite First Aid

Assume all snakebites in the wild are from a Venomous Snake.

Do Not Wash the Bitten Area

Do Not Try To Capture Snake unless a Registered Authorized Snake Catcher.

Do not move the victim let the medical help come to you.

Rest the bitten victim; lay them down on the ground keep all parts of the body at same level and cover with a blanket, jacket or anything on hand to help prevent Shock.

The individual may feel disoriented and dizzy. If dizziness does occur lay the individual down on their back and raise knees about 8 to 10 inches depending on comfort to aid blood flow to the brain.

Lowering the limb or bitten area will cause swelling and discomfort

Keep the person calm reassuring them that it's going to be fine.

When someone goes into shock, his or her skin becomes clammy, cold and pale.

Call ambulance in Australia phone triple zero (000) or from a mobile phone call 112.

In USA Phone 911

Apply a Pressure Immobilization Bandage to the bite site a 5cm bandage is recommended for arm and 7.5cm bandage is recommended for leg limbs. If you don't have a bandage on you use a shirt or any other material you can obtain to do the job.

First apply bandage to bitten area, then down to fingertips or toes and back up whole limb.

Apply the bandage as you would for a sprained, it needs to be secure enough to for support however you do not want to cut off circulation. The victim may become restless if bandage is to tight therefore keep an observant eye on the tightness of the bandage.

Snake venom travels through our Lymphatic System that is connected to our muscles therefore keeping the person whom has been bitten still and calm is vital for recovery.

Try to obtain calmly any relevant medical conditions the individual may suffer.

Observe the victim closely and report any changes to the ambulance crew.

It is fully recommended that anyone associated with snakes do a first aid course for self-awareness and peace of mind.

Cold-Blooded

As mentioned, snakes are cold-blooded animals, meaning during the cold winter months, they stay underground to keep their body temperatures warm. In fact, to help warm the body temperature, snakes will search for a place to hibernate that is lower than the frost line.

This might include a tunnel created by some type of burrowing animal, ant mound, or rock crevice. Known as a **Hibernaculum**, snakes will return to the same winter den annually.

Cold-blooded animals are not capable of producing their own body heat. Because of this, they also do not eat as much, as warm-blooded animals. In fact, when in the wild, snakes typically eat ever two weeks during the warmer months.

They also have to rely on the sunlight for heat, which is why in captivity, keeping your snake's cage at optimal temperature is imperative.

CATCHING A SNAKE – Get help from an expert!

People often find snakes in their yard, slithering around flowerbeds and in gardens.

If you find one and want to catch it so it can be released somewhere other than your yard, you need to call a snake catcher. This way, your garden is protected and the snake gets a new home.

Do not try to catch a snake by yourself. Call a snake catcher! If you live in an area that is constantly infested with snakes, and you feel it necessary to be able to handle the snake catching yourself in an emergency, you should attend **venomous snake handling training delivered by expert snake handlers.**

Courses are available in most countries. You can check here for courses **www.snakehandlers.com.au** Australia Wide. Check local state for information on courses available.

Interesting Species

Cobra

The Cobra is typically found in Southern China, Malaysia, India, Vietnam, Indonesia, and the Philippines. In all, there are six species of the Cobra to include the Naja, Water, Tree, Shield-Nose, Ringhal, and of course, the King Cobra.

We are all fascinated with the King Cobra and its ability to raise its head, open the shield, and look very imposing. The long, round scaled body tapers to a pointed tail, the top of the head is flat, and the two eyes beady and black, giving this snake its powerful look.

What happens is that when a King Cobra feels afraid or threatened, the ribs in the neck will flatten out. Then, the folds of the skin expand, which creates the famous hood. With the expanded hood and hissing sound, the Cobra definitely earns respect.

The King Cobra is the best known of all species, being known as the longest venomous snake in the world, often reaching to 18 feet long. This type of snake is more active during the day, being excellent climbers. Although the King Cobra prefers time on the ground, they will often resort to following prey into tall trees.

In addition, Cobras are great swimmers, leaving prey few places to hide. The male Cobra will use a neck wrestling technique to fight for his favorite female.

Once the snake wins the battle, it will then court her. The King Cobra actually has short fangs, which are designed to strike in a downward thrust and with 100% accuracy. The fangs are hollow, allowing the poison to pass through.

Then, with the King Cobra being able to raise one-third of its body, as high as four to five feet from the ground, you can see why this snake is so dangerous, so much that it is capable of injecting large enough quantities of poison to kill an elephant.

The interesting thing about Cobras is that most often, they would rather escape than strike. Although they appear aggressive and menacing, this is their way of protecting themselves. However, Cobras kill very few people, preferring to eat on live snakes instead, along with frogs, insects, and rats.

INTERESTING FACT: Cobras can only strike in a straight downwards that is why you see street entertainers kissing them on the top of their heads from behind, as they cannot strike from this position.

Anaconda

Many people have interest in the Anaconda, partially because of movies that depict them as some kind of monster. In fact, the Green Anaconda is a beautiful creature.

The Anaconda also bites different from other snakes. For them, they lunge forward but they also have the ability to strike from the side. As you probably know, the Anaconda can grow quite large, often longer than 16 feet at maturity.

The weight of the Anaconda is also impressive, weighing more and having more girth than the majority of other snakes. This species of snake is nocturnal, preferring to move about at night. However, they will also slither about in the day. Depending on the species, some can live as long as 30 years. If an Anaconda were caught in the wild, you would need to be careful concerning several factors, which include:

Upper respiratory infection
Water blisters
Worms or other parasites
Reluctant feeders
Scaring

Resource Section

Australian sites

http://www.kingsnake.com/oz/
http://www.australianfauna.com/australiansnakes.php
http://www.snakehandler.com.au/
http://www.reptilepark.com.au/
http://www.outback-australia-travel-secrets.com/australian_snakes.html
http://www.australianexplorer.com/snakes.htm
http://www.australiazoo.com.au/our-animals/amazing-animals/reptiles/?reptile=boas_and_pythons&animal=woma_python
http://www.anaes.med.usyd.edu.au/venom/snakebite.html

You can see our complete list of references and resources by visiting our Snake Site at:

http://www.pet-snake-guide.com/

Section Two:

How to Simply & Easily Keep Your Snake Healthy

Snake Injury and Illness

As mentioned in the book, The **Ultimate Guide to Snakes**, snakes are just like any other pet on that they require proper care. When provided with proper food, bedding, heat, lighting, water, and handling, your snake will remain healthy and strong.

However, snakes can be faced with a number of challenges to include things such as poor husbandry, infected snakes, and so on.

In this bonus book, we have provided you with some of the more common types of illnesses or injuries your pet snake may be faced with, the cause or causes of the problem, and solutions for helping your snake feel better. After all, a healthy snake will provide you with years of enjoyment. Therefore, since snakes cannot care for themselves, it is up to you to ensure your snake has everything needed for a long, healthy life.

Abscess

Symptoms

Unhealed and infected wounds
Puss around the infected area

Causes

Bites from prey (mice/rat)
Puncture wounds (caused by sharp objects or bedding in the cage)

Solution

Abscesses can be internal or external. The external abscesses are spotted by the white, cheesy substance around the wound. However, internal abscesses are more difficult to identify. Typically, you would notice the snake not eating, reduced activity, constipation, and an overall appearance of being ill.

Due to the pus substance, treatment with topical ointments is difficult. For an internal abscess, a veterinarian would need to open the wound surgically, and then flush it out prior to antibiotic treatment. For an external abscess, a pus specimen would be cultured to determine the best antibiotic treatment, usually administered by injection.

Blister Disease

Symptoms

Pink to red appearance on the bottom-most scales
In later stage, swelling and infection of the scales

Causes

Dirty, damp cage

Solution

At the first sign of Blister Disease, you want to have your snake treated by a veterinarian. Standard treatment would involve both topical and injectable antibiotics. To prevent Blister Disease from becoming a problem again, the snake's cage would need to be cleaned and sanitized on a regular basis.

Cancer

Keep in mind that reported cases of cancer in snakes is rare but it can occur.

Symptoms

Tumor growth
Unhealed wounds
Lethargy
Lack of appetite

Causes

Unknown

Solution

Remember, tumors found on a snake can be benign or malignant. Therefore, if you find a lump or mole, do not panic. While all species can develop cancer, Boa Constrictors seem to have a higher rate of incidence. If you notice any of the above symptoms, schedule time with your veterinarian so a biopsy can be taken to determine if the problem is in fact cancer.

Cloacaliths

Symptoms

Dehydration
Constipation
Lethargy

Causes

Dehydration (causing urinary excretions to dry out)

Solution

When the snake becomes dehydrated and urinary excretions dry out, uric acid stones can develop with the Cloaca. The result is that urinary waste and feces is impossible, causing the snake to become ill. Although dehydration can be the cause of Cloacaliths, there could be an underlying problem so we recommend your snake be treated by a veterinarian.

Inclusive Body Disease (IBD)

Symptoms

Neurological disorder, presenting as flopping head to one side, slow or awkward movement, gazing aimlessly, seizures, regurgitation, pneumonia, leukemia, and more)

Causes

Retrovirus (mites help spread this disease so the affected snake should always be quarantined)

Solution

Unfortunately, there is no known cure for IBD. Therefore, if our snake shows such symptoms, and is diagnosed with IBD, the only fair thing is humane euthanasia.

MOUTH ROT

Symptoms

Swelling around the mouth or labial scales
Open or scabbed over sores around the mouth or labial scales
Puss filled pockets inside the mouth
Cotton like patches inside the mouth
Mouth cannot close completely

Causes

Bacterial infection (caused by feeding in a cage with shavings or wood bark, rotting wood, rodent bites during feeding, unsanitary cage, spoiled food, etc)

Solution

If the problem is caught early enough, you can easily cure Mouth Rot at home. For this, you would take a Q-tip dipped in antiseptic such as Listerine (50% water and 50% antiseptic), rubbing it on the

137

affected area. Other antiseptics that work well include hydrogen peroxide and Betadine.

This would need to be done about three to four times a day until the infection clears up. Just make sure the Q-tip is only damp and not sopping wet. If the infection is not treated, the jawbones can be affected. If you notice the infection still present after one week of home treatment, then the snake will need to see a veterinarian for the administration of antibiotics.

Nutritional Deficiency

If your snake is not feed on a proper schedule or if the snake were, sick and not feeding, then you could experience a problem with nutritional deficiency. If not corrected, the snake could become very ill and even die. Keep in mind that snakes are designed by nature to go for long periods without food but if your snake does not accept prey longer than two weeks, you need to start looking for signs of anorexia.

Symptoms

Refusing to eat

Causes

New snake (needing time to adjust to its new home)
Pre-shedding period
Later stage of pregnancy
Older snake, which does not feed as often as a younger snake

138

Newborn snake
High strung species
In hibernation period
Hyperactive (breeding season, newly acquired, etc)
Obesity (self diet)
Ill or injured

Solution

If the snake will not eat, you want to try to supplement the diet, which can be done with vitamin and mineral injections. Another option is to implant a gelatin capsule filled with powdered vitamins and minerals. You also want to make sure your snake has a clean and sanitized cage, new bedding material, fresh water, food, and that the environment is correct as far as temperature and humidity levels.

Interestingly, while all of these things can help encourage feeding, the most common reason a snake in captivity will not feed has to do with a lack of safety. If your snake does not have adequate visual security and places to hide while feeding, it might stop eating. As mentioned, something as simple as vegetation, rocks, or a hiding box will do the trick.

Finally, make sure you understand your snake species natural requirements.

For instance, if you have a snake that loves to burrow in sand or dirt, then you would need to ensure the cage has sand or dirt. If the snake loves

139

dense vegetation, then make sure it has dense vegetation. The more you can match the cage's environment to that of the snake's natural environment the better the feeding process will be.

Other tips you might try include:

Feeding your snake at a different time of the day or evening. If the snake is nocturnal, being more active at night than in the day, be sure food is offered during its alert time.

Reduce the amount of handling

Rub the prey over the snake's nose and around the mouth or tap the prey lightly in the same areas

Although not usually recommended, offer your snake live prey or if the snake typically eats like prey such as the Boa Constrictor or Python, switch to pre-killed prey.

Try feeding your snake in a different, more private cage than the cage in which it lives:

Choose smaller size food
Try different types of food

If all else fails, see the veterinarian (may have to force feed the snake with a special, flexible tube).

Parasites

Symptoms

Parasites are broken down into three categories:

Intestinal (Endo), which are found in major organs
Crawling (Ecto), which means crawling around or on
the outer skin
Subcutaneous (Burrowed), which means under the
skin

Regurgitation
Weight loss
Anorexia
Bloody stool
Runny, smell stool
Lethargy

Causes

Parasites can be caused by a number of things
depending on the type of parasite. For instance,
parasites can be brought in from bedding or
developed from rotten food, among other things.

Solution

Again, depending on the type of parasite, proper
treatment would be provided. Keep in mind that
many times, parasites are perfectly harmless and
will eventually run their course without the aid of
treatment. Therefore, if you happen to find larvae or
eggs in your snake's stool, you do not necessarily
need to medicate.

The following are a few examples:

Ticks - These parasites suck blood, which causes
anemia, spread of disease, and discomfort to the
snake. For these reasons, the snake would need to

be treated immediately. If not treated, the snake could actually die. In the case of ticks, use heated tweezers to pull them off but gently. When the tweezers are very warm, the tick will open its mouth, releasing the bite.

Mites – Although these do not feed on the snake's blood, they can carry disease and make your pet miserable. Unfortunately, since mites are so small, if you notice symptoms, you might need to have the snake checked by a veterinarian.

Worms – For some types of worm parasites, you could use one to two drops of a product called Ridworm in the water as a preventative measure (great for roundworms and hookworms). However, the snake's feces would need to be checked for larvae or eggs so again, if you suspect something is wrong, have your snake checked by a veterinarian.

Amebiasis – Considered one of the most common of all parasite problems seen in captive snakes, this contagious disease is caused by a single-cell organism called the ameba. When food and water becomes contaminated, the snake can easily be infected. With laboratory examination and samples of feces, a veterinarian can confirm the diagnosis and then treat the snake with antiprotozoal medications.

Trichomoniasis – This common parasite is often seen in the feces during normal examination. This parasite comes from eating mice and rates that are harboring the parasite. Although gastrointestinal

142

disease to include vomiting and diarrhea are the common symptoms, sometimes this is hard to spot. If you have more than one snake, they would all need to be treated with the appropriate antibiotic and/or antiprotozoal medication.

Paraphimosis

Symptoms

Hemipenes protruding from the base of the tail for an extended amount of time and not going back in

Causes

Prolapsed organ

Solution

Your snake would need to be seen by the veterinarian at which time he or she would properly clean and put the prolapsed organ back in place. In most cases, the organ can be sutured into place with success, removing the stitches in about two weeks. However, if the organ were severely damaged or if it prolapses often, the veterinarian may need to amputate it. Keep in mind that this will not affect urination since the snake does not urinate through the hemipenes.

Prolapsed Organ

Symptoms

Not eating

Lethargy

Dull eyes and skin

Causes

Straining from uric acid stones

Straining during egg laying

Parasite infestation

Intestinal disease

Unknown

Solution

When a prolapsed organ occurs, one or more of the snake's organs invert inside out. In some cases, the organ will actually protrude through the external opening. Although the exact cause of the prolapsed organ may never be determined, your snake needs veterinarian care.

Respiratory Infection

Symptoms

Excessive yawning

Breathing with the mouth open

Bubbles coming from the mouth or nose

Wheezing

Sticky mucous

Clicking sound when breathing

Regurgitation

No appetite
Lethargy
No tongue flicking

Causes

Low cage temperature
Improper humidity levels
Exposure to other animals with respiratory infection

Solution

Since snakes are not capable of coughing or sneezing, if the cage has humidity levels that are too high, it could cause pneumonia or actually cause the snake to drown in its own congestion. Therefore, if your snake shows signs of a respiratory infection, never increase the humidity. Instead, increase the heat to the highest setting allowed for that species. If your snake has started to regurgitate, encourage water but do not feed. If you notice the skin being loose, then chances are your snake is dehydrated.

In this case, place Pedialyte in its water bowl in place of the water. When the symptoms cease, reset the temperature to the middle setting and offer food.

If the snake does not get better, have it checked by the veterinarian.

Rostral Abrasions

Symptoms

Sores, scrapes, or open wounds around the nose

Causes

Repeated attempts of escape

Solution

While trying to stop your snake from using its nose to try to open the lid of the cage is not always possible, you can make sure your snake has adequate hiding places, lots of vegetation, and rocks. Just make sure any branches or vegetation is low so the snake cannot use them to reach the top of the cage.

You might also consider buying a deeper cage, which makes reaching the lid impossible. Unfortunately, if the snake continues this action, it could lead to deformity. While this does not harm the snake, it does alter its appearance.

Septicemia

Symptoms

Anorexia
Lethargy
Dehydration
Regurgitation of digested food
Red skin and scales
Bleeding from the skin

Causes

Internal bacterial infection (via abscess or wound from serious injury) – associated with reproductive tract, gastrointestinal, and/or respiratory

Solution

If you suspect your snake has Septicemia, you need to seek immediate care.

Unfortunately, recovery is usually poor but treating with the appropriate antibiotics quickly is the best option for recovery.

Thermal Burn

Symptoms

Burned skin patches (first, second, or third degree)
Puss on open wounds

Causes

Hot rocks – Very simply, never use hot rocks in a snake's cage
Exposed light bulbs
Ceramic heaters (inside the cage)
Under Tank Heat (UTH) Pads with too little bedding material

Solution

The first step would be to remove the source of the problem. Then, follow the same treatment for Scale Rot, keeping in mind that to completely renew its

147

skin, your snake may have to shed two or three times. If the burn is severe or deep, see a veterinarian for tissue removal and more intense antibiotic treatment.

VIRAL INFECTION

Symptoms

Lethargy
Anorexia
Dehydration
Problems with digestion, respiratory, and nervous system

Causes

Unknown

Solution

Unfortunately, viral infections in a snake are extremely difficult to identify and then treat. Making matters worse, the majority of viral infections are highly contagious, which is why we always recommend you quarantine any new snake for two months prior to putting in the same room with an existing snake.

Additionally, when handling the two snakes, you would need to make sure your hands, equipment, or anything touched is carefully washed to avoid spreading the infection.

Scheduled Veterinarian Care

The best thing you can do for the life and wellness of your snake is to ensure it is seen on a regular basis by a Herp veterinarian. By knowing the possible injury and illness that your snake might experience and keeping up on regular checkups, you should be able to enjoy your snake for many years.

During a physical examination, the veterinarian would perform a fecal examination, do blood work, microbiologic workup, and provide your snake with a good, overall exam. We recommend your snake see a veterinarian annually unless a problem arises.

With this, you can help prevent disease, keeping your snake healthy and happy.

Remember, identifying and treating problems early is the key to a healthy pet. During this physical examination, your veterinarian will ask you specific questions to include:

How long have you owned the snake
Where did you purchase the snake
Do you know about the previous owner
Do you own other snakes and if so, what kind

What size and type of cage is the snake kept in
What type of bedding do you use
What other features are included in the snake's cage
Do you use a heat source and if so, what type
What type of lighting do you use
What type of food are you giving the snake
How often is the snake eating
Does the snake regurgitate
How is the snake's activity level
What temperature do you keep the cage
Does the snake defecate regularly
When did the snake shed last and were there any problems
Is the snake drinking okay
Does the snake appear alert

Tips For a Healthy Snake

As you will discover, maintaining a healthy snake is not that difficult. With proper care, your snake will live a long, happy life with few to no health problems.

Understand the Species

Remember, every snake species is different. Therefore, if you own a Boa Constrictor and want to buy a Green Snake, you would need to know specific information for both, as it would vary. The more you know and understand your snake the better! This means learning requirements for feeding, housing, temperature, handling, etc.

Husbandry

Each snake has very specific needs pertaining to housing and bedding.

Some snakes love to lie on rocks in the open while other snakes need places to hide. Make sure your snake has proper space and the proper environment within the cage.

Diet

Your snake will need fresh vegetables and the appropriate meat for its diet.

We STRONGLY recommend you use only pre-killed mice and rats, which are then frozen and thawed when time for feeding, which will help reduce the risk of parasites.

The only exception might be for constrictor type snakes that generally prefer to kill their own prey. However, if you can get the Python or Boa to feed on pre-killed food, we recommend that first.

Hot Rocks

Although we said it before, we want to say it again – **NO HOT ROCKS**.

Unfortunately, hot rocks are advertised as the best way for a snake to enjoy a heated nap. However, hot rocks are notorious for causing burns, thus serious injury. Therefore, use a different type of heat if needed.

Clean and Sanitary

Yes, we mentioned this one too but it is critical that your snake's cage be clean and sanitary at all times. A dirty cage harbors bacteria that can be very harmful to your snake so the cleaner the better! When cleaning the cage, use 10% bleach and 90% water for the inside and outside of the glass.

In addition, any other exposed area should be sealed with waterproof sealer so you do not have rotting wood or the growth of bacteria. Finally, make sure your snake's bedding is changed on a regular basis and that it is provided with fresh water daily.

Herp Veterinarian

Once you buy your snake, locate a reputable Herp veterinarian that caters to snakes. Remember, a Herp veterinarian is not like a standard veterinarian.

This individual has gone through specific training for reptile and amphibian medicine. While a regular veterinarian could probably help in an emergency, we strongly recommend you find a reputable Herp veterinarian prior to buying your snake.

Section Three

Successful Snake Breeding

Breeding Your Snake

Breeding snakes is a fun project. The process of breeding and then watching baby snakes hatch, is self-gratifying.

Whether you plan to breed your snake as a family project or for profit, you want to know exactly when to breed, how to breed, proper care, best environment, and more, which is what you will find in this bonus book, "Successful Snake Breeding".

Keep in mind that while these guidelines will help get you started, breeding snakes in captivity is kind of a hit and miss adventure. For starters, you will find that breeding responses or the reproductive cycle of most snakes is prompted by average temperatures experienced, and the length of the day versus length of the night.

Typically, snakes become more sexually active after they have come out of winter dormancy, sometime in the spring when temperature and length of day versus night are optimal.

Therefore, to be successful with breeding your snakes in captivity, you want to make sure they have some level of winter cooling and then warming first or changes of success are slim. In fact, some snake species such as the King Snake, Bull Snake, Rosy Boa, and Rat Snake require longer cooling than species from tropical regions.

Snake Preparation

To get your tropical and many temperate snakes ready for breeding, you want to start by separating the males from females. Then, stop feeding your snake for two weeks prior to the cooling phase. You would then need to lower the relative humidity, along with the temperature in the snake's cage.

For the daytime, you want temperatures to fall between 78 and 83 degrees and at night, between 69 and 73 degrees unless specified different for your species of snake. This cooling period should be maintained between 60 and 90 days, with the recommended timeline more like 90. Keep in mind that most breeding experts recommend the male's cage temperature be slightly less than the female's cage.

Now, during this cooling period, you can provide your snake with natural day and night time light. In fact, you could keep the area dark if you want, which many experts believe to be best. Then, because of the cooler temperatures, your snake's digestive system would slow down. Therefore, you want to cut back on the number and frequency of

156

feeding. You may even find that your snake has no interest in food at all during this time. Once you have reached the 60-day mark of the cooling period, begin to warm your snake with equal hours of natural day and night. Just make sure that the cage's temperature is maintained around 75 to 78 degrees and then during the day, 78 to 80 degrees. When the cooling period is over, put your snake back in its normal cage or environment with optimal temperatures. The snake's body will warm naturally over the course of two to four days at which time you would want to offer it a meal. For this, be sure the prey is small. Once the snake takes the small prey, the next feeding could include normal sized food.

Now, if your snake did not eat during the "hibernation" or cooling period, you want to make sure the snake is at its perfect weight prior to going into this phase and then in the spring, fed heavily. The female will then begin to shed after the hibernation period, at which time she should be placed in with the male.

Although each set of snakes are different, some will begin the courtship process immediately.

Courtship

The courtship among snakes is quite fascinating. For instance, the male snake may locate a female only to find that other males are staking their position nearby. However, males will generally ignore competition while they move forward with the courtship rituals.

There are some males that will put up a fight, engaging in ritual combat dances while the bodies intertwine as they try to force each other's head down. In most cases, the larger of the two males wins. With the exception of a few venomous snakes, the interesting thing is that the two males will seldom bite one another.

During courtship, males will rub the undersides of the head along the back of the female to stimulate and then orientate his body to her body. For copulation to occur, the male must lift the female's tail using his tail although Pythons have special spurs to accomplish this. As mentioned, males have hemipenes (two penises) found on either side of the body.

These hemipenes contain small sacs, which are found at the base of its body.

Mating

If the snakes show no interest in each other, you may need to provide a gentle misting to help stimulate the natural reproductive behavior. Simply use a spray bottle, pointing the nozzle upwards so the "gentle rain" falls down on the snakes.

Another option is to place another sexually mature male in the cage but keep in mind that some breeds such as the Python and Boa will fight. Therefore, this option for stimulation would need to be done with great supervision and care, being prepared to separate the snakes at any moment. Chances are, your snakes will breed immediately, but to make sure, we suggest you allow them to stay in the same cage with each other for about 7 to 10 days.

During the mating process, one of the hemipenes is inserted into the females

Cloaca

To help hold the hemipenes in place, most snakes have tiny spines to help. The process of copulation generally takes a few minutes although it could take several hours. Then, the female will take more than one mate, as well as mating with the same male more than one time.

When the copulation period is over, injected sperm is stored in a tube-like oviduct for about two months. At that time, the female releases large eggs from her ovary. Interestingly, each has a very large yolk, which is then fertilized by the stored sperm. Once fertilized, the eggs funnel to the cloaca where they are released and deposited in a hole in the ground, in a log, or under a rock.

For some snake species to include the Diamond Python and King Cobra, the female snake will make a nest for the eggs using vegetation. Then, the female stays with the eggs, guarding them with her life against predators. To help the eggs develop, the

159

female Python will twitch the muscles that resembles shivering.

You will also find some snake species such as the Flowerpot Blind Snake, which is capable of reproducing without going through the mating process. In this case, the females reproduce through parthenogenesis in which the chromosomes within an unfertilized egg replicate. Then, the embryo develops, just as if it had been fertilized through normal copulation.

Once the snakes are hatched or born, it will take two to four years for them to reach maturity. For those in captivity not battling the elements of the wild, life span is between 15 and 30 years. Unfortunately, in the wild, snakes die relatively young due to disease or predator attack.

If you have one snake that seems very eager to mate and the other that appears totally, disinterested, we recommend you introduce the male to the female's cage about every three days. This process could take months in that sometimes, you simply have to get the two snakes on the same page. While this is relatively rare, it does happen. Remember, some females may not breed for a year or two so if she does not take to the male, you might have to wait a year and try again.

Copulation

All you have to do is leave them alone and let nature takes its course. Once the female becomes impregnated, eggs will grow inside her. Now, you can breed your snake any time of the year but for the best results, we suggest spring. If you want to breed in the winter, you would need to take a few steps to encourage breeding.

Make sure the cage temperature is between 55 and 65 degrees for about 14 weeks. However, to do this without harming the snake, you must take great care. This means both male and female would need to be cooled separate and gradually. To accomplish this, reduce the food so during the coolest period, food in not sitting in the snake's belly undigested, which could be fatal.

In addition, make sure your snake has plenty of clean water. After the cooling period, warm the snakes back up to optimum temperature, slowly so the snake's system is not shocked. Once your snake warms up, his/her appetite will explode, as they get ready to breed. With this, feed the snakes as much food as they want to consume. Next, put the two snakes in the same cage, introducing them for the breeding. While it might seem a little like spying, you need to pay close attention during copulation. The reason is that some snakes will have their tails beside each other or they might even have their bodies wrapped around one another but if you were to look closely, you might find copulation never occurred. Therefore, during this phase of the breeding, you will need to be patient.

Pregnancy

Once you remove the female, place her in a clean cage with damp moss where she will lay her eggs if pregnant. She will then lie on the eggs to keep them warm. The length of your snake's pregnancy once the eggs are fertilized is about seven weeks. At first, the female snake will continue to feed, as usually and in fact, you might want to supplement her for extra nourishment.

Then as the eggs grow, her appetite will start to decrease. At this time, you could still offer her food but go to pinkies or smaller prey that would be easier for her to digest. Remember, your female snake may stop eating altogether. Soon, you will start to see a change in her body, specifically the lower belly of her lower abdomen.

The belly will begin to look rounded and depending on the species of snake, some will shed just prior to the eggs being laid, such as the Corn Snake.

Typically, this would occur about one week prior to the eggs being laid. Even if the snake does not shed, you can usually tell when the snake is ready to lay the eggs by the way in which she acts. For instance, she will become more active during the day and at night, as she prepares a place for the eggs. In fact, she may look as if she were looking for a way to get out of the cage.

Clutching

Clutching, or laying eggs, is something some female snakes do over a period of days. In fact, double and triple clutching is quite common unless egg binding should occur. If you find that the egg-lay process is taking longer than 48 hours, you should contact your veterinarian in that she may be having problems.

After all of the bulges on her belly are gone and the final clutch is laid, the eggs should be removed. For this, take care that the eggs are not turned. In other words, pick them up just as they are, placing them in the clean cage the same exact way. After this process, the female will be lethargic, worn out from the process.

Hatching

With hatching, oblong, leathery-like shelled eggs are deposited in the environment where they incubate. When the embryonic development of the eggs is complete, the eggs will hatch, and tiny snakes emerge. If you want to hatch the snake eggs on your own remove them from the cage and bury them partially in damp vermiculite around 82 degrees.

You will notice the young eggs feeling soft and with an almost leather-like feel, which is normal. In addition, during the incubation period, it is common for the size and shape to change. The key in hatching snake eggs is keeping them moist and warm. Then, when you remove them from the egg-

163

laying chamber to set them in the incubator, be especially careful.

The most important part of this step is to make sure the top of the egg stays on top or the egg will die. If you want to rebreed the snakes immediately, you can. For hatching, the eggs will produce life in 60 to 90 days. If you want to incubate fertile eggs artificially, you would simply add a small amount of water to an empty Styrofoam chest.

Then, place a thick layer of peat moss, vermiculite, shredded newspaper, or sphagnum moss on top. Carefully place the eggs onto the medium and moisten the material just slightly. The goal here is to ensure the eggs do not dry out but also that they not become too moist.

For this to be successful, a proper level of humidity is required, usually between 75% and 85%. Cover the chest, placing it on a standard house, heating pad that has been turned on and set on the lowest possible temperature setting. The key here is to get the Styrofoam chest to a temperature around 75 to 85 degrees.

Then, you would maintain the proper level of moisture of the medium for 55 to 60 days at which time baby snakes would emerge.

Live Births

For hatching, the snake will have fertilized eggs inside the body. When the embryos are fully developed, they are born live. Live births occur in about 20% of all species. However, you would find live births most often in colder regions, which helps the female control the temperature of the eggs inside her, as they develop.

The pregnant snake will lie in the sun while keeping the eggs warm. This action helps speed up the rate of development so the young snakes are born prior to severe cold. In addition, live births can be highly advantageous to some snakes that live in warmer climates. As an example, you will find that Sea Snakes give birth to live young, which prevents them from having to come to shore to lay eggs, where predators would have better access, making the eggs more vulnerable.

Without doubt, watching your snake's eggs as they begin to pip is an exciting time. You would notice the eggs beginning to dimple about a week prior to the actual hatching due to the neonates beginning to ingest the yolk in the egg, which is all part of the preparation process. Pipping occurs when the neonates slit the eggs with a special egg tooth.

As the eggs begin to split, the snake's tiny nose would emerge. Remember, getting outside of the hard shell is a big process for a small snake.

Therefore, the baby snakes will slowly work their way out, resting for hours during the process as needed.

165

However, they will soon make it to the outside world. At this point, the snake will be attached by the umbilical cord. Allow this to detach naturally in that removing it too early could actually kill the baby snake.

Caring for Neonates

The neonates or baby snakes usually hatch within 48 hours of each other. All you have to do is take care of the new hatchlings until you are ready to find them or give them a new home. After being born, neonates need special care. The average clutch is about 20 eggs. Therefore, you could end up with quite a responsibility until you have homes for your snakes so you need to be prepared.

We strongly suggest you purchase a hatchling tub, housing each of the neonates separately, which will allow you to monitor the baby's progress more effectively. With neonate snakes, you need to keep a schedule of when they slough, go to the bathroom, eat, and so on. By keeping a journal on each of the snakes, you would be able to know if they ever regurgitate or show signs of not doing well.

One of the most challenging factors associated with a newborn snake is stress.

Therefore, it is essential that you avoid or eliminate any level of stress possible.

That means paying close attention to the neonates, making sure the temperature of their environment is correct, that they are being fed, have fresh water, clean bedding, and so on.

For bedding, use a soft kitchen towel, not shavings, or wood chips. The neonate's skin is still very tender and young so you need to provide them with a soft bed. In addition, a soft kitchen towel will allow you to keep the snake in its hatchling tub for feeding, which again takes some of the stress out of moving the snake too early.

Provide the snake with clean water daily and make sure they have a place to hide.

If the hatchling tub is small, then push the towel up in one corner so the snake can climb under. If the hatchling tub is larger, then you might be able to fit an empty toilet paper roll. In addition, you want to provide the snakes with an environment that has a warm end and a cooler end. The best way to accommodate this is with a heat strip on the bottom of the cage. Simply place it on one-half of the cage so you get the two temperature zones.

Following stress, the second most challenge aspect of neonates is feeding. To get the baby snakes to feed, you will need to be persistent but also patient. By assisting the snake, you should do quite well. However, you may need to try several feeding methods until you find one that works best for the species of snake you have.

The most important thing is to work slowly and with great care. Typically, most snake hatchlings will eat a small, pre-killed pinkie after the first shed.

Remember, snakes have a natural instinct that they will follow. However, if you have a new snake that is not feeding, we can provide a few suggestions to get the feeding process started.

First, make sure the cage is at the optimal temperature for the species of snake you have. In addition, you want to provide the snake with a hiding place, comfortable bedding, clean cage, and so on. Other tips that could help the neonates feed include:

Do not handle the pinkie with your hands. Instead, use tweezers.

Prior to placing the pinkie in the cage, warm it up slightly, increasing the natural smell, making the pinkie appear live rather than dead. For this, simply blow the pinkie with a warm hairdryer for a few minutes.

Try feeding the neonate snakes at night with low lighting. Since most snakes are nocturnal, meaning they are more active at night, this will usually do the trick.

If the snakes are not responding to these feeding methods, it could be that the snake does not realize the pinkie is food. Without movement of the prey as the snake would see in the wild, it simply does not register. Therefore, you could use tweezers to wiggle the warm pinkie, giving the impression of live movement.

When doing this, you want to avoid wiggling the pinkie directly in the snake's face, which would be an annoyance. Most often, the snake will strike. As soon as it has hold of the pinkie, release your hold and let the snake eat. You may need to try this technique several times before it works.

Now, if you have exhausted all of these methods without success, you could then move to adding scent to the pinkie. Anything like the scent of a live mouse or rate, fish, chicken, frog, slough, or newly shed skin are all good options. Even the scent of an ordinary garden slug will work.

Finally, if your neonate snake has not eaten in the first six weeks of life, you might need to assist feed. Unfortunately, this method is stressful to both the snake and to you but critical to keep the snake alive. For this, take the head of a pinkie and with your fingers only, force the head gently into the snake's mouth.

To ensure success without causing injury to your snake, follow these steps:

Lift the snake gently, moving it so its head is between your thumb and two forefingers. Let the body rest behind, using your little finger against the palm of your hand, which provides stability.

Next, pry the mouth open, using the tip of your finger. Just use a little force while being gentle.

Now, quickly slip the pinkie head into the mouth, putting it in nose first.

Push the entire pinkie head down the snake's throat, which takes a little effort and unsettling, especially the first time you try it.

After the pinkie head is in the snake's throat completely, shut the mouth and gently massage the pinkie further down into the body.

Finally, put the snake back into the hatchling tub or cage, allowing it to have some quiet time. At this point, the snake will either swallow the pinkie or regurgitate it.

Nesting Box

You want to make sure your snake is offered a nesting box. Some females will use it and some will not but she should have the choice. This will provide her with a safe, private place to lay her eggs, helping her to calm down. As she begins to lay the eggs, most will be out without a few hours. During this time, leave the snake alone, allowing her time to go through this natural process.

Although you could offer the female some food at this point, she may or may not have enough energy to eat. However, use her favorite food in that you need to encourage her to get some nutrition in her body. Additionally, provide her with supplement food at this time.

Breeding Behavior

It is important to keep in mind that some snakes will become highly aggressive during the breeding season. Therefore, to avoid being bitten or wrapped by the snake, you need to handle it with extra care. If you have a larger snake such as a Python or Boa, we suggest you take even more care due to size. While proper handling is important throughout the breeding season, you especially want to be patient and gentle when introducing the two snakes.

While some female snakes will breed every year, not all do. In fact, some will only ovulate every two to three years, something you see more often with larger, live-bearing boa constrictors. In addition, once the mating session is over, which could take two to four days to complete the two snakes should be separated and then fed a good, hearty meal.

Breeding Life Span

Typically, a female snake will stop producing good eggs around age 10, although this does vary slightly from one species to another. If you want to breed your snake ongoing, producing neonates annually, you would need to consider this age factor. With this, as the female reaches age seven, you might want to choose a younger, healthy female to take her place.

For the male snakes, they generally will breed a year or two longer than the female but again, you could follow the 10-year rule. As you have young males born, you might keep a couple of them as pets or breeders so as the male reaches old age, he could be put out to pasture so to speak and replaced with the younger studs.

Summary

We want to thank you for purchasing "*The Ultimate Snake Owner Guide*." We enjoyed putting this information together for you so when you get ready to buy your first snake or add more snakes to your existing collection, you will have all the information needed and then some. Snakes are magnificent creatures that are to be respected for their ability to survive in a challenging world.

As you have read throughout this book, owning and caring for a snake is a sometimes challenging but always a rewarding adventure. We have made every effort to ensure the accuracy and completeness of the content provided in this book.

However, the author or any other person associated with this book makes no warranties or guarantees, expressed or implied, regarding errors or omissions and assumes no legal liability or responsibility for loss or damage resulting from the use of information contained within.

Additionally, the author or associated persons do not guarantee, expressed or implied, for the accuracy, completeness, or usefulness of any information, apparatus, product, or process disclosed, or represents that its use would guarantee improvement or success in relation to subject written.

Any reference herein to any specific commercial products, process, or service by trade name, trademark, manufacturer, or otherwise, does not necessarily constitute or imply its endorsement, recommendation, or favoring.

Finally, the content of "*The Ultimate Snake Owner Guide*" is copyright protected, with all rights reserved and may not be copied or imitated in whole or part without first requesting and receiving full written permission from the author.

Again, thank you for allowing us to take you into the wonderful world of snakes.

Don't forget to visit our snake website at:

http://www.pet-snake-guide.com/

Feel free to leave your feedback on this book and any questions you may have about snakes in general.